The RV Buyer's Survival Guide

How to Survive and Profit through the RV Buying Experience

Learn how to buy an RV from a 20 plus-year RV Industry veteran

- Types of RV's
- Determining your Real Needs
- Customer Preference Worksheet
- First Time Buyers - Know before you go
- Narrowing the Field
- Comparison Shopping Guide – Motorized
- Comparison Shopping Guide – Towables
- When is the Right Time to Buy?
- Understanding the Selling Process
- Selecting a Dealer and Salesperson
- How a Manufacturer figures MSRP
- Understanding Trade-in Values
- Negotiating the Deal / How the Desk Works
- The Finance Department
- Taking Delivery Expectations and Realities

By Bob Randall

Published & Distributed in the United States of America by:
RV Savvy Productions Inc.
3969 Stedman-Cedar Creek Road
Fayetteville, NC 28312-7496
www.rveducation101.com

The RV Buyer's Survival Guide, Edition III
Copyright © 2007 by: RV Education 101

Third Paperback Edition

Library of Congress Cataloging-in-Publication Data

RV Buyer's Survival Guide, Edition III

First American Edition
printed and bound by
RV Publications.com 2000

Second American Edition
printed and bound by
Central Plains Book Manufacturing 2002
ISBN 0-9706928-1-1

Third American Edition
printed and bound by
United Graphics Inc. 2007
ISBN 0-9776025-3-2

Author: Bob Randall
Editor: Mark J. Polk
Photos: Courtesy of RVIA, www.rvia.org
Cover designed by Cary Hyodo, www.gnuink.com
www.rveducation101.com
www.rvuniversity.com
www.rvpublications.com

"There is nothing like traveling in an RV, exploring this great country and creating wonderful memories and experiences to look back on in the future. Saving money on the purchase of your RV is an added bonus to this great lifestyle. Enjoy the book!" ~ Bob Randall ~ author

CONTENTS   PAGE

FOREWARD

My name is Mark Polk and I am the owner of a company called RV Education 101. We produce educational videos on how to use and maintain RV's and I am the author of *"The RV Book" & "The Insider's Guide to Buying an RV"*

When Bob Randall asked me to proofread and edit the third edition of *"The RV Buyer's Survival Guide"* I considered it an honor and a compliment. I have written in depth on the subject of buying an RV, and consider myself knowledgeable, from an insider's perspective, on the RV buying process.

While reading and absorbing the content of Bob's guide I realized I was seeing the RV buying process through another set of eyes. Through the eyes of a person who experienced the process from a manufacturers viewpoint and then again from a RV dealers viewpoint. I found the information in this guide to be extremely interesting and straightforward, offering insightful ways to save a great deal of money during the RV purchase. Bob also offers a method for making sure the consumer gets the "right" RV to meet their specific needs.

If I had to sum this guide up in one sentence it would go something like this; if this guide was priced at $500.00, Chapter 6 alone would pay for itself!

I would recommend this guide to anybody in the market for an RV. Bob's years of experience in the RV Industry and knowledge in the RV buying process will save the savvy RV buyer a great deal of money on their RV purchase.

Happy Camping,

Mark J. Polk
www.rveducation101.com

INTRODUCTION

Congratulations. If you are reading this guide, you are likely preparing to take a major step forward in your life by joining the many millions of others who have discovered the RV lifestyle. Being an RVer in today's society is partially about escaping the realities of our everyday lives, but it's also about enjoying the beauty of our magnificent country at your own pace - and doing it in your very own rolling home. It's not about scrambling from one motel to another, from one strange bed to another, or from one plastic meal to another. RVing is about traveling with all the comforts of home. It's about freedom!

To truly enjoy this lifestyle, you must first have the means to seek the dream - the RV. At first thought, you might say, "No big deal. I'll just go buy something and then hit the road." Hold that thought! This can very well be your first step toward a nightmare that's repeated day in and day out in every corner of America. RV buyers sign on the bottom line without getting the best deal and the right RV. These people envision an RV as their ticket to adventure and serenity. And with this lofty dream in mind, they walk blindly into an RV dealership - so consumed by their dream that they ignore one stark reality: that without the proper knowledge of what they are doing they can easily, and inadvertently, hand over far too much of their hard-earned money to someone who may not have their best interests in mind.

The purpose of this guide is to properly prepare you to make an informed purchase. In some instances, an RV can cost as much, if not more, than your home - the kind *without* wheels! Most of us buy and trade our automobiles every few years. And with only a relatively few car manufacturers to choose from, there is a great deal of information available. So we most often come away from a purchase satisfied. However, unlike an automobile, which serves primarily to get us from point A to point B, an RV serves as a "home" that goes to all points of the compass.

There are literally hundreds of RV manufacturers building a mind-boggling number of RV brands. Most offer dozens of floor plans in each brand. With the help of this guide, you will be able to sort through the nearly countless choices and determine what is right for you. And, then - and only then - the "insider" information in this guide will provide you with the ammunition you'll need negotiate a fair price.

There is no reason you should feel lost and confused as you take the first steps in the search for this better lifestyle. Whether you are brand new to RVing, or are an experienced trader, there is information here that will enlighten and reward you in many ways. Buying an RV is not just about what you pay for it. It's about making sure that you get what you pay for, and that what you get is what you need.

So take about two hours to carefully read this guide. You bought it, so read it. If you calculate how much you'll likely save with this new knowledge, you'll earn in savings the equivalent of thousands of dollars per hour. Now, how often do you get an opportunity like that short of winning a lottery? Once you have done this "homework," you will be ready to start your search with the confidence that you will not be "taken," but will have the tools necessary to negotiate the best deal.

Oh, one last note about recent changes in American attitudes since the tragedy of September 11 2001. The disaster we all witnessed on that day has had many side affects on all of us, some bad, and some good. One of the more positive affects has been a tremendous desire by many to rediscover and enjoy what America has to offer us here at home. This desire coupled with the RVs perfect ability to help in that quest, has sent the RV Industry off on another period of boom times. In the years since then, this has had both a good and bad affect for potential buyers. The good being, a more focused attempt by manufactures to build more and better RVs to meet that new need and demand. The bad being **_some_** dealers trying to excessively profit off that new need and desire. Buying large ticket items has always been something you should approach with both eyes wide open, and with knowledge a forehand.

I hope in your reading of this guide, that we can open your eyes wide in understanding the RV buying process ....Before you open your checkbook. Good luck & good shopping

Bob

ABOUT THE AUTHOR

The author, like many of you, is also a "Baby Boomer" and has spent most of his working life in the recreational vehicle industry. He started camping with his family in the 1950s and went into the RV business in the early '70s. He spent his first few years working as a Customer Service Manager, and later, sold RVs. Over the next twenty years, he moved up to the position of Director of Sales for the largest manufacturer of recreational vehicles in North America. After more than two decades in the industry, he retired and began a career at the retail dealer level - helping customers find the "means to their dreams." Through his many years associating with RV owners, he met many happy and excited RV consumers and many prospective buyers. Unfortunately, over those same years, he also heard many horror stories from disenchanted customers who had suffered nightmarish experiences while trying to find their dream RV. Most of these bad buying experiences could have been avoided if the sales person had been more concerned with the customer's "true needs" instead of trying to sell them the "Special of the Week" for the highest commission. Many of the horror stories told to the author, by these dissatisfied RV buyers, wouldn't have occurred had the customer understood the RV buying process. In other words, they caused their own problems. Unlike buying a car, where there is a wealth of information available - including annual reviews and ratings in magazines like Consumer Reports - the would-be RV owner has a hard time finding quality information. So it's much easier to fall victim to a bad deal.

That's where this guide fits in. If you put into practice the "insider" knowledge here, you will have a much more positive and rewarding experience. Whether you are just starting out on the RV lifestyle or simply extending the trip as an existing owner, there is much you can learn and profit from by reading this manual.

Since its first printing many years ago, the guide has been read by tens of thousands of potential RV buyers. Based on the hundreds of thank you e-mails and phone calls we've received from "New RV Owners" we know it has saved untold dollars in excessive "asking prices." For some more great RV information after the sale please take a few moments to visit www.rvuniversity.com after reading the guide.

GLOSSARY OF COMMON RV TERMS

The glossary below reflects terms used in the RV world. These will come handy when trying to communicate what you are looking for. As you go through the literature about RVs that dealers will provide, it should help you understand more about the coaches and of the buying/selling process.

AIR RIDE SUSPENSION: When units utilize air bags as part of the suspension to help the smoothness of the ride and control of the ride.

AIR LEVELING SYSTEM: When a unit utilizes an air bag system to level the unit during set up in lieu of mechanical jacks, which touch the ground. These are generally computer operated.

ALUMINUM FRAME CONSTRUCTION: When the RV framing is made of aluminum as opposed to wood.

ARTIC PACKAGE: An RV that is equipped with additional insulation and heated holding tanks for cold weather camping.

BACK UP CAMERA: A camera mounted on the rear of many motor homes. The monitor at the cockpit allows you to see what is behind you, the same as a rear view mirror in an automobile. These cameras sometimes have audio available too.

BASEMENT STORAGE: Large enclosed outside storage areas located between the frame and the floor of the unit. Some will offer these areas with heat to prevent water from freezing during use in times of colder climates.

BATTERY DISCONNECT: Also called a "Kill Switch," this is used to disconnect the battery power to the coach when it's not in use to prevent parasitic drains on the batteries.

BLACK WATER HOLDING TANK: A tank mounted under the RV that collects water and waste from the toilet. When the tank is ¾ or more full it is emptied or dumped into an approved dump station or campground sewer. The black water tank is treated with chemicals to control odor and assist in breaking down waste.

BUNKHOUSE: Bunk beds as a part of the sleeping arrangements. These style units are generally designed to sleep 6 or more people. Many bunk beds are rated for a maximum of 150 pounds.

BUS MOTOR COACH: A large motor coach, built on a commercial bus chassis or rear diesel pusher, generally with a square front end design and are diesel-powered.

CHASSIS: The undercarriage of the RV. It can be either purchased or produced by the manufacturer and is the foundation of a new home away from home. (Take special note of this item)

CITY WATER CONNECTION: A water connection on the outside of the RV, used when you have an external water supply, such as at a campground. A potable water hose is used to connect the water supply to the city water connection on the RV.

CLASS/Type A: This can be either a gas- or diesel-powered motor home -full height, built on a specialty chassis, fully self-contained, from 21' to 45' long. The amenity level of a Class A can vary greatly by price point and size. (See types available).

CLASS/Type B: The term describes a camper van unit, built on a van chassis, which sometimes can be self-contained. These are often thought of as multi-use family vehicles. (See types available)

CLASS/Type C: Built on a modified truck chassis, fully self-contained, from 19' - 31' long. These generally offer the greatest amount of flexibility in sleeping arrangements. (See types available)

CLASS I THRU V HITCHES RECEIVERS: Weight ratings of hitch receivers designed to carry what you are towing. What's required depends on the unit weight, hitch weight and the type of tow vehicle. A great resource for learning more about these topics is the Trailer Towing, Weights, and Hitch Work & Backing DVD & E-book available at www.rveducation101.com

COCKPIT: Simply put, this is the driver's area of the motor home.

CONVERTER: refers to the device which converts 110-volts AC power down to 12- volts DC power for items in the RV requiring 12-volts.

COUPLER: The front part of a travel trailer or pop up tongue that attaches to the ball mount of the tow vehicle.

DELAMINATING: When the fiberglass panel separates from the luan backing used to construct fiberglass sidewalls on an RV. This is usually caused by water damage.

DEMAND WATER SYSTEM: A secondary water system you use when not hooked up a campground water source. A 12-volt water pump pressurizes potable water stored in the fresh water holding tank. The pump cycles on and off as it senses a demand for more water. i.e. When a water faucet is opened.

DESK or DESKING: This is the term used at the dealership when referring to the manager working the numbers on a pending sale. This is where the real dollars are saved or spent.

DRY WEIGHT: Dry Weight (DW) or Unloaded Vehicle Weight (UVW) is the actual weight of the RV as built at the factory. The DW does not include passengers, cargo, fresh water, LP gas, fuel or after market accessories.

DIRECT SPARK IGNITION (DSI): is a system used to ignite the burner on a propane appliance with the touch of a button. It is commonly used on RV refrigerators, furnaces and on some water heaters.

DUCTED AC & HEAT: When the A/C and heat is supplied throughout the RV using a ducting system. A/C is ducted in the ceiling and the heat is ducted in the floor.

F & I: Refers to the finance and insurance department at the RV dealership. We have devoted a section to this later on, it is very important to read even if you are paying cash for your unit.

FIFTH WHEEL TRAILER: A trailer with a raised front end, that extends over the bed of a pickup truck, or custom tow vehicle. A special hitch is mounted in the bed of the truck, over the rear axle, to tow a fifth wheel trailer. Fifth wheels are frequently referred to as a fiver. (See types available)

FLIP SOFA or JACK KNIFE SOFA: Describes a convertible sofa that folds out to make a sleeping area, usually 44" to 46" wide when folded out.

FRESH WATER HOLDING TANK: A tank mounted under or in the RV that stores potable water for use while traveling or dry camping. To pressurize the system and use the water in the holding tank you turn the 12-volt demand water pump on.

FULL HOOK-UP: A full hook-up means you connect the RV to the campground electric, water and sewer facilities. In addition to this it may also include cable TV and phone line connections.

GENERATOR: Commonly used on motorhomes, a generator produces 120-volt AC power. A generator allows you to use 120-volt appliances when you are not plugged into an external electrical source. Generators are rated in kilowatts. For example a 5 KW generator is 5,000 watts.

GRAY WATER HOLDING TANK: A tank mounted under the RV that collects wastewater from the sinks and shower. When you dump or empty your holding tanks you should always dump the black tank first, then the gray tank. This will assist in rinsing out the flexible sewer hose.

GALLEY: As in water-going vessels, the kitchen area of the RV.

HARD WALL CONSTRUCTION: Refers to the exterior wall construction. This is usually a laminated construction term used for units with fiberglass sidewalls.

HITCH RECEIVER: The hitch receiver is mounted to the frame of the tow vehicle. The ball-mount slides into the receiver. There are five classes of hitch receivers based on the maximum amount of weight the receiver can handle.

HOSE CARRIER BUMPER: Many manufacturers allow for the sewage hose you will need for emptying the holding tanks to be stored in the rear bumper between uses. Some use separate storage areas found elsewhere.

INVERTER: An electrical device that changes 12-volt DC power into 120-volt AC power. It is used to power 120-volt appliances or electronics such as a microwave or TV when you don't have access to an external 120-volt power source. The amount of power that is available depends on the storage capacity of your battery(s) and the wattage rating of the inverter.

KING PIN: The front portion of the fifth wheel. This is the attachment that is hooked to the trucks "In bed hitch" for towing.

KING PIN STABILIZER: A stabilizer tripod, which can be mounted under the king pin for added stability when the RV is parked.

MH: Abbreviation for motorhome.

MONITOR PANEL: Allows you to check or monitor the fluid levels in the gray, black and fresh water holding tanks. You can also check the condition of the auxiliary battery(s) and on some monitor panels the propane level.

MOTORIZED RV: As implies, an RV not requiring a tow vehicle, most often a Class A, B, or C motor home.

MSRP: Manufactures Suggested Retail Price. These prices are normally found on sheets posted in or on the RV on a sales lot. Their purpose is to add credibility to the price. After all, you have to start somewhere.

NADA BOOK: The RV edition of the National Automobile Dealers Association (NADA) book is used by RV dealers to determine used RV values.

OEM: Abbreviation for Original Equipment Manufacturer

OVERHANG: The portion of the motorhome that extends from the rear axle to the rear of the motorhome.

OVERHEAD SLEEPER: Refers to the sleeping area found in the front end of either a Class C motor home or a truck camper.

PAC: Term that describes the percentage over invoice that the RV dealer adds to an RV sales price to help pay for cost associated with selling it (i.e. rent, advertising, etc.)

PARK MODEL: A non-self contained unit which is intended to remain stationary for the most part (see types available)

PDI (Pre Delivery Inspection): Term used to describe the inspection of the unit and systems prior to delivery to the buyer.

PINCHED ROLLED: A term describing the method of sidewall lamination where adhesion is accomplished by squeezing the walls together to bond them.

POP-UP OR FOLDING TRAILER: A tent trailer with greatly expanding sleeping areas, usually twice the size opened as when closed. (See types available)

PUSHER: Refers to a rear engine motor home, most always diesel-powered. (See types available)

RECREATIONAL PARK TRAILER (RPT): An RV trailer designed to be taken to a location such as a campground or resort area and set up permanently. A park model trailer has more household type features and amenities than a conventional travel trailer. (See types available)

RV: Abbreviation for Recreation Vehicle. A Recreation Vehicle combines transportation and living quarters for recreation, camping, and travel. They can be classified in two basic groups, motorized RVs and towable RVs. Motorized RVs include Type A, B and C motorhomes. Towables include pop-ups, travel trailers, fifth wheels and truck campers.

RVDA: Recreation Vehicle Dealers Association

RVIA: Recreation Vehicle Industry Association

RV QUEEN BED: Term used in RVs for a certain mattress size. Not actual 60" X 80" queen, generally 60" X 74" or 76" long. Fitted sheets can be expensive and hard to find.

SELF-CONTAINED: This means you have your own systems for power, water, heating, electricity, toilet and cooking facilities. You can make do without outside connections for a limited amount of time - a few days or even a week depending upon your use.

SLEEPER DINETTE: This is a booth dinette that can be converted to a sleeping area when needed.

SLIDE OUT: An expandable room that slides out to provide extra living space when not traveling. Slide outs can be powered by hydraulics or electric. Modern day RV's often have multiple slides on units, and they greatly add to your living space.

SOFT SIDE or CORRUGATED CONSTRUCTION: Defines exterior wall construction, generally non-laminated surface material of metal or fiberglass.

SPLIT BATH: Describes a bathroom arrangement where the bathing areas are separated from the toilet facilities.

SPORT UTILITY RV or SURV: Hybrid travel trailer with hard sides and expandable bed ends similar to a pop-up.

STABILIZER JACKS: Defines jacks added under the frame or chassis which aid in the leveling and stabilizing of the unit while parked.

STICK & TIN: An RV with wood framing and corrugated aluminum exterior.

TAG AXLE: A second rear axle that aids in the support of the extra weight in the rear and handling of the motor home.

TOWABLE RV's: Term used to describe a non-motorized recreation vehicle. Includes travel trailers, fifth wheels and pop-ups.

TOW BAR: Tow bars are used to tow a vehicle behind a motorhome when the vehicle is towed with all four wheels on the ground.

TOW DOLLY: A trailer used to tow a vehicle behind a motorhome when the vehicle cannot be towed with all four wheels on the ground. Two of the vehicles wheels are on the tow dolly and two are on the road surface.

TOY HAULER: An RV that has a ramp door on the back and cargo space to load motorcycles, ATVs or other toys inside.

TRAVEL TRAILER: A self-contained trailer usually 15' to 40' in length. (See types available)

TRUCK CAMPER: A unit that mounts in the bed of a pick-up truck and sleeps 2 to 6 people. They can be totally self-contained or only partially so. They range from 8' to 13' in length. (See types available)

TT: Abbreviation for travel trailer.

TV: Abbreviation for tow vehicle.

VACUUM BONDED WALL: This is where all the components of the walls are put together and a vacuum is pulled to ensure air is not trapped inside the wall. Generally, it produces a stronger wall. But it's more expensive to fabricate.

WALK THROUGH BATH: This is where the aisle runs through the center of the bathroom, as opposed to the room being off the main aisle.

WET BATH: This is when the shower area is also the area that houses the commode and sink. Generally only found on small units and truck campers.

WHEELBASE: The distance between the centerlines of the primary axles of a vehicle.

WIDE BODY: This describes the width of the unit. A wide body will have a width of 102" as opposed to a standard width of 96". Some states still have restrictions on the use of the wider units as to where they may travel.

CHAPTER 1
TYPES of RV's

The types of recreation vehicles available on the market today are as varied as the people who use them. They cost as little as a few thousand dollars for a new tent trailer (pop-up), to a million dollars (plus) for a custom-designed luxury bus. This guide focuses on the nine basic types that compose the majority of recreational vehicles in the marketplace. Obviously, pre-owned units are available in all these categories and we will speak later of things you should be aware of when shopping for a good used unit.

NON MOTORIZED RV's
POP-UPS / TENT TRAILERS

For many new RV buyers, especially young families, this is the first step to RVing once they decide to start enjoying the great outdoors. These affordable units are simple to use, set up and maneuver. They require a minimal tow vehicle - the family car, van or SUV will normally do.

A tent trailer is just what its name suggests - a tent attached to a trailer box. They come with many options and floor plans. A <u>basic</u> tent trailer will provide a sitting area, a sleeping area, and that's about it. Other more deluxe units include a kitchen, shower, and even a toilet in some cases. A major appeal of a tent trailer is its small closed dimensions while on the road compared to the open size when in use. A unit 10' long, when closed, will expand to 18' when opened. The 3' height while towing expands to 7+' high when opened. The low profile in the closed configuration makes this an ideal unit for RVers who have never towed before, as it is easy to back up, pull or turn around. Your dealer can generally provide you with a tow hitch that attaches to your vehicle. Because of the light weight, hitching and unhitching is a simple one-person job.

Most pop-up manufacturers offer what I refer to as an entry-level line and a deluxe line. Some of the differences are in construction such as the roof and lift system, the size, and in how they are equipped. Options available for some pop-ups are air conditioning, refrigerator, water heater, furnace, dual LP gas bottles, inside or outside shower, upgraded interiors, awning, screen room and electric brakes. Top-of-the-line units may also include an interior bathroom for maximum privacy while camping.

Pop-ups are commonly referred to by their box size. What this means is the length of the box that is mounted to the frame of the trailer. For years, manufacturers offered 8-foot, 10-foot and 12-foot boxes for their pop-ups. Now innovative manufacturers are coming out with even larger versions, 14-foot boxes, and off road models for campers that really want to explore America's back roads. The closed length of a pop-up is measured from the front of the tongue to the rear bumper. Pop-ups can sleep up to eight people depending on the model and prices can range from $5,000 to over $13,000.

TRUCK CAMPERS

A truck camper has many advantages for its owners, depending on the way they plan to use it. The greatest of these is that you basically have a small motor home when you need it, and your truck is free the rest of the time when not attached.

This makes for a very versatile RV that can access back roads and remote areas other RVs can't get to. Truck campers are often times the choice for avid outdoorsmen and women. It provides all the benefits of other RVs and still allows you to tow a boat, motorcycle trailer or horse trailer behind the truck.

Today's truck campers are available in many different sizes and floor plans. They are built in 8, 9, 10 and 12 foot plus models. They come equipped with kitchen facilities, dining areas, bathrooms, and sleeping arrangements. Many manufacturers are making these campers more spacious by extending the cab-over area and adding small slide-outs. Slide-outs are designed to provide more living space inside an RV.

Numerous options are available to include air conditioners and generators making the truck camper fully self-contained. You need to have a truck that is capable of carrying the weight of the camper. When you're not using the camper it can be removed from the truck.

The camper unit itself comes with jacks (either manual or power) to make loading the camper on or off the pick-up easier. The quality of construction of a truck camper is generally in proportion to what the unit costs. The least expensive units have a wood frame construction with sheet metal siding. More expensive units feature an aluminum frame with laminated fiberglass exteriors. Again, as with most things in life, you can get as little or as much as your pocketbook will allow. Sleeping capacities vary with the size of the unit. However, most will sleep between two and six people. Prices start at about $6,500 for a basic unit and go to more than $23,000 for a fully loaded model.

TRAVEL TRAILERS

Travel trailers today are very specialized compared to those of the past. Travel trailers have always been thought of as a part time home built on a chassis that you tow where you go. This is the only thing about trailers that hasn't changed through the years.

Today, travel trailers are designed to fulfill the needs of RVers with different lifestyles, tow vehicles and planned use. Some units are lightweight, which allows for less powerful tow vehicles. Others include everything from washers and dryers to whirlpool spas, several slide outs, and are aimed at fulltimers. Travel trailers, without a doubt represents the most complex portion of the RV marketplace. The last time I checked, there were over 130 brands being produced and sold in the United States alone. One large manufacturer produces nine brands, with over 200 floor plans and a choice of four interior colors, with many other available options.

Travel trailers can be an excellent choice for many people because they offer so much flexibility. One of the more popular features is the slide out, which adds a great deal of interior living space. Travel trailers, depending on size and floor plan, can sleep anywhere from two to twelve people.

With a little bit of practice, they are relatively easy to maneuver. Once you arrive at your destination, set up is easy. With the equipment available, such as power front jacks, stabilizing jacks and automatic awnings, set up may take only a few short minutes (You will, however, pay for all these, nice to have, labor-saving devices).

Generally, non-powered versions of the just-mentioned devices come as standard equipment, and can be less prone to malfunction. Construction of travel trailers runs the gamut of technology from what we call "Stick and Tin" to "Heli-Arc" aluminum frame with vacuum laminated fiberglass walls. Each method has its own benefits and advantages, such as weight, strength, repair-ability, cost, ease of maintenance, etc. Again, these differences will all factor into what you will spend for the travel trailer. The manufacturer most often will make the chassis rather than purchase it from a chassis builder. Once you hear a few sales presentations on the features and benefits of construction, you can then do some shopping on similar types of construction to find the unit that best suits your needs.

Travel trailers range in size from 15 to 37 feet and offer all the comforts of home. Most travel trailer manufacturers offer what I refer to as entry level models, mid-line models and high end models. Think of it like you can buy a Chevrolet, a Buick or a Cadillac. With today's lighter weight tow vehicles almost all manufacturers offer lightweight and ultra-lightweight versions too. Travel trailers can sleep up to eight people depending on the model and prices range from $10,000 to more than $50,000.

Another version of the travel trailer is the **Hybrid Travel Trailers.** The concept is a small, light weight trailer with pull-out or drop-down bed ends similar to a pop-up. These hard-sided trailers can be easily towed with today's smaller SUV's and provide much more space inside when they are set-up without having to raise and lower the roof. Hybrids are equipped with most of the same amenities found in conventional travel trailers. Hybrid trailers can sleep up to six people and prices range from $10,000 to over $ 25,000.

Still another addition to towable trailers is the **Sport Utility Trailer** (SUT), also referred to as toy haulers and Sport Utility RV (SURV). These trailers have living quarters in the front and cargo space in the back.

There is a rear ramp door that lowers so you can load your motorcycles, ATV's or other toys that you want to take with you. They offer cooking facilities, dining areas, bathrooms, slide outs and sleeping arrangements like conventional travel trailers.

There are lots of options available including generators, making the SUT fully self-contained so you can enjoy out of the way places. SUT's come in a variety of sizes to accommodate what the outdoor enthusiasts want to take along. The popularity of toy haulers lead manufacturers to build these in fifth wheel and motorhome models too, so prices can range anywhere from $15,000 to over $100,000.

The customer preference sheet, found later in this guide, will help you greatly when you actually start the shopping process. Travel trailers generally range in length from 15' to 40 feet. Prices start at about $10,000 and go to $40,000 and higher.

FIFTH WHEELS

5th Wheels are the ones you see that extend over the bed of the pickup or custom tow vehicle. Because of the bi-level design, fifth-wheels offer the most living space of any towable RV. They range in size from 17 to 40 feet. Fifth wheels require a special type of hitch to be installed in the bed of a  truck. The truck must be properly equipped and capable of handling the weight; this includes the weight placed directly over the rear axle.

The other benefit of this configuration is that by being pulled from the bed, versus the rear of a tow vehicle, the combined length of the two vehicles is shorter. For example, a 35' trailer has a 3' tongue (hitching part) and about 32' of living space. If hooked to a 20' truck, the overall length would be about 55 feet. A 35' fifth wheel has 35' of living space and, when hooked to the center of a 20' truck bed, the overall length would be about 51 feet. Hence, you save about 4' in length and pick up 3' in living space. Because you are getting more living space in a 35' fifth wheel versus a 35' travel trailer, you can expect to pay more. A good way to figure the cost is to look at comparable units on a "box length" cost, per foot basis. There are other costs associated with the chassis construction of fifth wheels versus a trailer because of the added weight being carried in the front end. Additionally, the "Pin Box," which is the hitching attachment on the front, is adjustable to fit a range of trucks.

Fifth wheels tow and handle better than conventional travel trailers and combined with spacious living quarters are often times the choice for fulltime RVers. Fifth wheels, like other towables, are available in entry level, mid-line and high-end models. Fifth wheel manufacturer's offer many different floor plans.

Two-thirds of all fifth wheels built today offer at least one slide out and most have multiple slide outs, increasing the already spacious interiors. Lightweight versions that can be towed by smaller trucks are also very popular.

Construction techniques vary from wood frame with aluminum siding to welded aluminum frame with fiberglass siding. Like most other RVs, fifth wheels offer kitchen facilities, dining areas, living rooms, bathrooms and sleeping arrangements. Optional equipment like generators, make fifth wheels fully self-contained. Since the debut of multiple slide outs, fifth wheel sales have become the fastest growing segment in towable RV's. Fifth wheels tend to be purchased by experienced RVers who have learned, over time, what their needs are. These RVs are generally loaded with features and cost more than other trailers. Lengths range from 17' to 40 feet. Prices range from about $12,000 to $120,000 and up.

RECREATIONAL PARK MODEL

Although not new in the RV industry, park models are starting to gain more popularity with RVers who spend a lot of time in one place. A park model is a cross between a travel trailer and a mobile home. The intent of this product is to serve as a semi-portable cabin. For the person who wants to get out and play without the hassle of towing or owning an expensive tow vehicle, these are the perfect solution.

For the most part, they are not designed to be self-contained or moved on a regular basis. They are more of a "destination" recreation vehicle. By this I mean that you park it for the season or years if you prefer, at your favorite location and then commute to it when you want to use it. They are more popular in the central & eastern part of the United States, where more private parks are available or where these RVs can be left on site year round.

Many are built by traditional RV manufacturers and marketed by RV dealers, but this is where the similarities end. When I say they are not self-contained, I am referring, for starters, to such items as multi-fuel refrigerators versus larger 110-volt home-style units they feature. It's also common for park models to have electric water heaters versus the LP ones found in other RVs, the absence of holding tanks for wastewater, and sometimes, no installed furniture. When looking at park models from a construction standpoint, they are a hybrid. They are generally not built to mobile home specifications as they pertain to snow loads, wind shear capabilities, insulation factors, etc. This is because they are not built with the intent of full time, year-round living.

However, you will find all types being made by many different companies. Generally speaking, the cost to manufacture this type of product is far less than manufacturing a comparable travel trailer or mobile home, and they tend to be very profitable items for dealers. So don't be afraid to do some hard negotiating on these.

There are 12 foot wide models that are usually around 36 to 40 feet long. This type has a peaked, shingled roof and siding like on a house or cottage. 12 foot wide models need to be moved by professionals with the proper type of equipment. The other type is slightly less than 8' 6" in width and up to 39 feet in length. This type looks more like a travel trailer and can be transported by the owner with a proper tow vehicle. They have slide outs to give additional living space when they are set up. Most park model trailers do not exceed 400 square feet and they are equipped with full bathrooms, kitchens, living room, bedrooms, heat and air, all appliances and most are fully furnished. Because they are designed to be stationary for the most part many RPTs have full size appliances like you would find in your home, rather than RV type appliances. Prices can range from $15,000 to over $60,000.

MOTORIZED RVS

Motorized RVs, much like towables, come in all sizes, shapes and prices. They can be basic or loaded with every feature you could want. For many RVers, "motorized" is the only way to go. As you will see, there is a coach to fit every need and pocketbook. Motorized RVs are categorized by the industry into three classes or types: Class A, Class B and Class C. However, for clarification, we will divide the Class A into two categories, gas-powered and diesel-powered since they are two very distinct products with two very different price points (ranges).

Again, I will start with the smallest and work toward the larger, more expensive units.

CLASS B MOTORHOME

A Class B or Type B motor home is more-or-less a van conversion. There are only a few manufacturers of the chassis portion of this motor home, although there are many conversion companies on the market. These motor homes are primarily designed as multi-use vehicles. They can be purchased with only a few amenities  such as a sleeper couch and icebox or fully loaded for full self-containment.

Many people consider these the perfect unit for tailgate parties or weekend outings at the lake. Then, on Monday morning, the owner can load the kids in for school and move on for the weekly shopping. Class Bs generally start with an extended van or what is called a van "cutaway" (just the cab portion of the chassis) and build up from there. Class B motorhomes are divided into a simple conversion using an extended van with modifications or a full cutaway conversion. The simple conversion can add tens of thousands of dollars to the cost of a standard extended van and can include raised roofs, refrigerator, TV, toilet, and cooking accommodations. Generally, though, there are no holding tanks, or very small holding tanks.

A cutaway conversion can be a full-blown RV with all of the above including bathroom with shower, generator, holding tanks, four-wheel drive and much more.

They are easier to maneuver and park, more fuel efficient, and can be used as a second vehicle. Class B motorhomes are popular among all types of consumers. They work well for one and two travelers, or they can make a great family vehicle. Some models can sleep up to four people. Lots of people use Class B motorhomes to tow horse trailers and boats. The length of a Class B is generally limited to about 23' overall. The simple conversion vans start at about $30,000 and the cutaway versions can run as high as $100,000.

CLASS C MOTOHOMES

This type of motor home is what many motor home owners begin and stay with - and for many good reasons. The greatest is its size versus function followed closely by the ease of driving. To truly understand when I say "size versus function," you almost need to have been in one.

The manufacturers of Class Cs, for the most part, do an excellent job of packing the coach with everything necessary into a very compact package. Class C motor homes generally come generator-ready, with the option of adding one later if you don't want one initially. If you believe, however, that you will add a generator any time in the future, your best bet is to include it with the new RV. You will be money ahead and the generator will be covered under the warranty.

The Class C, in many cases, will sleep more people than many of the larger Class A motor homes. For this reason alone, Class Cs tend to be the RV of choice of many campers, especially families. Much like a folding trailer, they offer good value if you are trying to take a bunch of folks camping for as little money as possible. When you look at a Class C, your first thought might be that it looks like a fifth wheel box on a motorized chassis. You're not too far off. A Class C utilizes the front over cab area for a sleeping area of considerable size. A fairly recent development is an option where this area can be used instead as an entertainment center with TV, stereo, CD/DVD player, etc. Depending on the size of the unit, you will find additional sleeping areas in a fold-out sofa, a flip-down dining area, and a queen bed in the rear. Thus, you can sleep 6 to 8 people in as little as 26 to 31 feet.

There are more and more Class C motor homes with slide outs, and not just in longer models, but in models as short as 22 feet. Class C motor homes can be purchased with as few amenities as you wish to keep the cost down, or as many as your budget will allow.

I have seen many folks keep Class Cs for a few years while their children are young and then trade up to a Class A after they move away, when they have more time to travel. Other RVers will only own a Class C motor home, no matter what.

As I stated earlier, one of the reasons that many RVers will always consider this their motor home of choice is its "drive ability." Although driving a Class C can sometimes be a challenge in a heavy wind (as with most RVs because of the height and mass) they are no more difficult to drive than the family SUV or a pick-up truck.

They feature automatic transmissions, power steering and other functions of a typical automobile. This is particularly nice if a normally shotgun-riding spouse is willing to share the driving duties. Class C motor homes are most often found with either a Ford chassis with a V10 engine, or most recently with the GM chassis with a Vortec engine. Optional on some brands is a diesel engine. Class C motorhomes are manufactured in lengths ranging from 19' to 32' and range in price from $40,000 to over $100,000.

CLASS A GAS POWERED MOTORHOME

The Class A motorhome is how most non-RVers envision a motor home. A Class A is a full box-style vehicle where the driving area is fully part of the motor home, unlike the Class C where it is somewhat separated. Class A motorhomes either come as a straight side coach or with slide outs.

It's getting more difficult to find models without slide outs in today's market. When determining whether to purchase a gasoline-powered Class A or one with a diesel engine, you must first determine how you will use the coach.

A diesel-powered coach costs considerably more for several reasons, but if those reasons are not important to you, a lower priced gas-powered coach may make more sense. One major benefit of a diesel engine is longevity. A gas engine, properly taken care of and driven correctly, is usually good for 150,000 to 200,000 miles. After that, you are looking at a major overhaul or possible engine replacement. Diesels, however, are known to go several hundred thousand miles with only regular servicing.

So, how many miles do you think you'll **really** put on your coach? The second factor to consider is raw power - not just horsepower, but torque.

The torque difference is most important when you do two things: pull heavy loads and climb big hills or mountains. If you are not planning to spend your time climbing the Rockies on a regular basis or pulling anything more than a small tow vehicle, you probably don't need the added torque a diesel engine offers.

Adding to the cost of a diesel motor home is its transmission. Take for example the common Allison six-speed automatic, which has proven itself over many years. Also a diesel motor home costs more due to the chassis under the coach; it's substantially heavier than those under most gas Class A motor homes, with heavier running gear (axles) and larger wheels and tires and air ride suspension systems. These are just a few of the major items that can make a diesel-powered coach cost tens of thousands of dollars more than its gas counterpart. For most owners, a Class A gas-powered coach will do the job well and satisfy 99% of their requirements. If the time comes when they'll spend more time on the road, then they might be inclined to move up to a diesel-powered coach. With some of the improvements to the gasoline RV chassis in recent years the price for some higher end gas models is about the same as an entry level diesel model.

A Class A motor home provides significantly more under-coach storage then a Class C. Many have what is called "Basement" storage. This is simply a space left between the floor of the coach and the chassis. In addition, they have what is called "Saddlebag" storage, where the storage compartments are attached to the chassis rails of the coach. Many manufacturers have become quite creative with the basement storage area in terms of functional use.

The most popular application is the containment of the holding tank and water tank systems. This not only protects them from road hazards, but also helps to protect against soft freezes. To be protected against a hard freeze, the compartment needs to have some type of ducted heat, which is available on some brands and models.

Most Class A motor homes come standard with a generator of some type. Make sure it will run both air conditioners if the unit is so equipped. In a gas coach, the generator will be either LP gas or gasoline-powered. Gasoline is preferred. The coach's electrical power (110 volt) is provided by one of two sources, generator or shore power. Shore power is used when the RV is "hooked up" to external power, the electrical cord attached to the power center of the RV, which is equipped with a 30 or 50-amp service. If you have a choice, select an RV with the 50-amp service. There are electrical adapters that allow you to plug into services as low as 15 amps.

In many RV brands you will find what is called an "EMS" or Energy Management System. With EMS, the circuits needed to keep running during a power overload will be determined automatically. An example would be if both A/C units are running and you turned on the convection microwave oven to cook. The system would sense the overload and turn off the rear bedroom area A/C while you cook. When you are finished, it will restart automatically.

When you enter a Class A, you will immediately notice the feeling of openness in the coach. Depending upon size, they usually have a great room-type effect of being open, yet with defined living, cooking, sleeping and personal areas. The galleys are fully functional with everything needed and can include items such as convection ovens, side-by-side refrigerators, food processors, etc. The dining areas are set up as either a booth that converts to a sleeping area or a freestanding table. The living room and bedroom area may or may not include a slide out room. Either way, you will have a sofa that converts into a sofa sleeper. You will sometimes find a second sofa or love seat, but generally, you will have a rocker or recliner instead.

The bath area will most likely have a tub/shower combination, separate sink, and wardrobes. There are several different terms used to describe the bath layout arrangements. There is the walk through, in which the main aisle goes through the room. This generally has privacy doors on both ends. The side aisle bath is where the bathroom is offset from the aisle and completely private. The split bath arrangement separates the shower/dressing area from the area with the commode. There is also a walk through bath version that features a separate private commode room. Less often found anymore are the rear bath models.

The master bedroom will most likely have a queen bed. However, if you are tall, be aware of what RV manufacturers call an "RV Queen" bed - a full 60" wide, but only 74" or 76" long. Many brands, however, do have full 80" long queens, but be aware of what you are looking at. The important thing is that you must purchase special RV sheets to fit an "RV Queen" and they can be expensive and sometimes hard to find. RV beds are not the normal queen size because of the demands on the manufacturer to make everything fit, taking size and weight into consideration.

If it sounds like I just described something the size of a house, you're right. It's amazing how well most manufacturers have done at fitting all the amenities of a regular home into a relatively small space.

You can find all this in Class A motor homes as short as 28 feet. However, you will have to make compromises on shorter units. Shorter motor homes normally have what is referred to as a corner bed. This is where the bed is built into the corner of a wall, thus making it a bit difficult for the person on the inside to get out of bed when the other person is in bed. It is also more difficult to make-up a corner bed. Class A gas motor homes range in length from 21 to 38 feet. Prices range from about $50,000 to $200,000.

CLASS A - DIESEL POWERED

If you did not read the section above titled Class A Gas - please read it first. As mentioned there, the decision to purchase a diesel motor home, also known as a "Pusher" since the engine is in the rear, is one that you need to evaluate based on your needs and how you plan to use the coach. Diesels are an excellent investment in motor home ownership if the use factor is there. They generally will last considerably longer than a gas coach with the same time in service. Also, down the line, you will find the resale value can be higher as an overall percentage.

They do, however, cost more to purchase for some of the reasons mentioned above. Service can also be more expensive than with a gas powered unit.

Diesel motor homes, by virtue of their heavy-duty construction, are intended for longer, more demanding use. They are generally recommended to people who RV fulltime (six months and/or many miles a year), based on the coaches' durability and long life. As I mentioned earlier, there are quite a few additional items that are different and more expensive than in gas coaches. For this reason, and because these units are usually better suited for more experienced owners, they generally have more "creature comfort" features as well. Most have 50-amp electrical service and other standard options not standard on a gas coach. One item that may be optional and well worth requesting is a diesel generator. Another popular option that many RVers consider well worth the extra money is a hot water/ room heating system which is available in several brands. This provides you with both your heat and your hot water and is diesel-powered. This means you will only be using LP gas for cooking and as a back up fuel for the refrigerator.

As covered in the previous section, torque is what diesels are all about. When you climb a hill with a diesel, you get there quicker and with a lot less strain.

Also, if planning to pull heavy loads, such as a trailer, the diesel is the only way to go. When you start looking at diesel-powered coaches, one thing you will quickly notice is the variation in horsepower. In new coaches you will see that they range from 260 hp to 500 hp. Again, what is right for you depends how you intend to use the coach. The smaller 260 hp engine often comes with an Allison 5 speed transmission. Others mentioned above will have an Allison 6 speed transmission. With the exception of lighter duty use, the larger horsepower units are where you need to be. Keep in mind that today's gas model engines are well over 300 horsepower. When determining the required horsepower, look at items such as gross vehicle weight and gross vehicle weight rating. Then divide the weight by the horsepower. Once you have the horsepower in reference to pounds, do the same with the torque. Now you're looking at it from the "apples to apples" standpoint. Diesel Class A motor homes range in length from 28' to 42' and cost from about $120,000 to upwards of $600,000.

The only units larger and more expensive than the above are bus conversions. Builders of these "rolling mansions" literally take a bus chassis and build a motor home on top. These are obviously one-of-a-kind and are designed specifically around the needs and wants of their owners. They are popular with celebrities and other well to do people. These coaches range in size from 40' to 45' long with prices from a half-million to a million dollars plus.

CHAPTER 2

DETERMINING YOUR "REAL" NEEDS

"I know what I want; I want an RV to chase my dreams.

Armed with this thought alone, you are in danger of spending a lot of money needlessly. The best offense is a good defense when it comes to making a serious purchase decision on anything. The old saying goes "Act in haste, repent in leisure." This is not what you want to go through. This is not to say that there are not quick ways to determine the right RV for you. There are, if you follow the right path. If you are already an experienced RV trader (trading every three years or so), you probably know your way around an RV dealership and its salespeople. However, if you are like 90% of the customers that take the plunge every year, it is an exercise you probably need to polish up. Lender reports indicate that RVs have a payoff time of about 60 months, yet the average loan duration is twelve years, even longer for motorized RV's. This means that people rarely pay off an RV - they end up trading it in. This is the subject for this section. The most costly mistake you can make when buying an RV is paying too much for it or not buying the coach that's right for *you!* The time you normally discover this is when you go to trade it in. If this happens within the first year, you are in for an especially rude awakening.

Before we get into "Determining Your Needs," let's take a minute to talk about RV depreciation. RVs are no different than any other vehicle that is purchased new. As soon as you drive it off the lot, it will depreciate. The day you take it home, it goes down about 15%. In the first full year, it will go down at least another 5%. After a few years, the coach will plateau and your balance owed will be in line with the value you feel the RV is worth. At this point, you will be in a good position to trade it in. However, the consequences of depreciation are only a major problem if you pay full MSRP (Manufacturers Suggested Retail Price - more about that later). Depreciation is figured based on what the unit *should have sold for, not what you paid for it.* By the time you put into practice what this guide has to offer, you should be covered for one or two years of depreciation. This is not to say that an RV is a bad investment.

Remember, you are not buying an RV to appreciate in value; you are buying it to enjoy a new lifestyle. If you are looking for an investment that goes up in value, see your Realtor or stockbroker.

However, with an RV, you can save thousands of dollars annually on motel charges, restaurant meals, airline fares, etc.

You will also have a nice tax deduction - that is, if you financed the RV and don't already own a second home. Most all RVs qualify for deductibility (see your tax advisor for details or call the IRS at 800-829-3676 and ask for "Publication 936 - Home Interest Deduction" and "Publication 523 - Selling Your Home"). Therefore, it is critical to ask yourself, "What do we really want this unit to provide us with?" To help you through this exercise, I have put together what we at the dealership call the "Customer Preference Worksheet." It's a simple form that you should fill out with your traveling partner. Not only will it help you narrow down the field of potential candidates (by working like a funnel), but it will also help you determine each other's expectations. Many times I have seen the husband or wife look at each other with surprised looks on their faces. One will express what he (she) wants and the spouse will say "You want what?" It is better to get any possible disagreements out of the way before you get to the dealership. This way, when you start shopping you will both be on the same page.

Don't be afraid to walk into the dealership with a copy of this form already filled out, and hand it to a salesperson. It lets him or her know that you have done your homework and are serious. The information you provide will not only speed up the sales buying process, which can normally be very time consuming, but it will allow the salesperson to better address your needs rather than simply directing you to the "Special of the Week." As you will see later in the section "How to Negotiate A Deal," any RV you select can, very well, be the special of the week. But when you first walk into a dealership, you'll want to keep your options open.

When looking to buy a new unit, make a few copies of the worksheet; fill one out when you first start looking, and then another one when you have done some comparison shopping. Another good place to keep notes is in the back of this guide in the notes section for quick reference later.

When looking to purchase a pre-owned unit, fill it out and then get going. You can, and will, have fun while shopping for an RV. If you follow the basic steps, and maintain control of the buying process, you will end up with what you want and at a fair price.

CUSTOMER PREFERENCE WORKSHEET-

NAME: _____

TELEPHONE #: _____

ADDRESS:

_____

_____

TYPE OF UNIT DESIRED: (Class A, Pop-Up, Fifth Wheel, etc.)

_____

NEW: __ GAS: __ DIESEL: ___ENGINE SIZE PREFERRED: _____

PRE-OWNED:___ ACCEPTABLE MILEAGE: _____

NO OLDER THAN: _____

LENGTH RANGE: _____ TO _____

SLIDE OUT or MULTIPLE SLIDES _____ (Yes or No)

MANUFACTURER, BRAND, MODEL (If you already know specifics):

_____

INTERIOR COLOR RANGE:

_____

(Fabrics and Wood)

ESTIMATED MILES TO BE DRIVEN PER YEAR:

_____

TOW VEHICLE INFO (If buying a towable RV):

_____

EXPERIENCE WITH RVs (Whether you have owned or not):

_____

CUSTOMER USE DATA WORKSHEET

FULL TIME: ___ WEEKS: _____ MONTHS: _____ PER YEAR

PRIMARY SLEEPING (Yours) QUEEN: ____ TWINS: ___

NO PREFERENCE: _____

OTHER SLEEPING AREAS NEEDED (Specify # adults or children)

_____

EATING ACCOMMODATIONS –

BOOTH OR DINETTE: _____TABLE & CHAIRS: _____

BATH PREFERENCE –

WALK THROUGH: _____ SIDE BATH: _____

PRIVATE COMMODE: _____

FULL HOOK-UP CAMPING: _____% TIME

OR SELF CONTAINED _____% TIME

(This helps to determine holding tank, fresh water, and generator needs.)

STORAGE NEEDS (both inside and out - i.e. golf clubs, fishing poles, clothes, pots & pans etc.):

_____

_____

_____

_____

EQUIPMENT REQUIREMENTS (air conditioner, generator, satellite dish, TVs, TV antenna, CD, DVD, Washer/Dryer, Leveling Jacks, etc.)

_____

_____

_____

_____

_____

_____

_____

SPECIAL NEEDS (Handicap requirements etc.)

_____

_____

_____

DISLIKES (be honest, this is very important, i.e. center kitchen, split bath, corner bed, fabric colors, wood trim):

_____

_____

_____

PRICE RANGE DESIRED:

FROM $_____   TO $_____

TRADE IN INFORMATION (Brand/Model/Year):

_____

MILES: _____ MOTOR: _____ LENGTH: _____

OPTIONS ON UNIT:

_____

_____

_____

_____

BALANCE OWED: _____ LENDER: _____

ACCT #:

_____

ADDITIONAL COMMENTS & NOTES:

_____

_____

_____

_____

_____

_____

_____

_____

_____

_____

Note: RV Education 101 offers instructional DVD's on the various types of RV's. You should purchase a DVD for the type of RV you are interested in prior to going shopping for your RV. This way you are better prepared to ask specific questions and you will have a working knowledge of how the RV's are equipped and how the systems operate. The DVD's are available at www.rveducation101.com or the mail-in order form at the back of this guide.

CHAPTER 3

FIRST TIME BUYERS - KNOW BEFORE YOU GO

I can always spot a first-time buyer on the sales lot. They either look nervous, like they are lost, or come in like a boxer with their dukes up. Hopefully, by the time you read and practice a few of the suggestions in this guide, you'll walk in with the confidence of an experienced RV trader. As a first-time new RV buyer you will immediately be overwhelmed by the multitude of different types of RV's and price points available to you. Determining what is right can be mind-boggling - to say the least. Generally speaking, most RV dealerships welcome first-time buyers because they are the least demanding (i.e. they don't know what they should expect). The dealership knows it stands to make a very good profit off you. However, as a first-time buyer, you are actually in the best position you will ever be in because you are dealing from a cash position. When I say "cash position," I mean you have no trade in vehicle to cloud the deal negotiations. If you are planning to finance the unit at the dealership, you have again strengthened your negotiating position. (More on this later)

As we will address later in the chapter "How the Desk Works," there are several areas where the dealership makes a profit on the sale. First is the profit generated on the selling price over dealer cost. Next is the profit on the trade allowance versus an ACV (Actual Cash Value of the trade). These two profit centers are called the "front side" of the deal.

An equal or greater amount of money is made on what is called the "back side" of the deal. This profit comes from financing the RV and add-ons like extended service contracts, payoff insurance, vehicle insurance, paint protection plans, tire guard plans etc. A well-run dealership with a strong F & I person can easily match or surpass the profit on the front side of the deal. As a smart first-time buyer, you must be aware of where the dealer will make money, so you can avoid paying too much.

Let's start with the asking price or MSRP if the unit is new. Keep in mind that either "asking price" or "MSRP" is a starting point and nothing more, not what you must end up paying. These numbers reflect a gross profit, large enough to show a customer with a trade in, an amount reflective of retail value on his trade.

In other words if the dealership is only willing to put $10,000 of real money in your trade, but the retail value of the trade is $13,000, there will be enough cushion in the MSRP to make it seem that they are allowing you $13,000 for your unit.

As a cash buyer, you can realistically expect to pay from 15% to 20% off the asking price (or MSRP). However, it is not a wise move to start discussing pricing until you find the unit that really fits your needs. Bringing up pricing in every unit you go into will only set you up for a fall. Many customers ask salespeople "How much can I buy this one for?" Or they try to calculate the average discount percentage. This is a mistake on the buyer's part. It is better to wait and not tip your hand until you are ready to actually negotiate the selling price. The information you volunteer early in the game can and will most likely be used against you.

"Success is when preparation meets opportunity." If you want to be successful buying the right unit at the right price, you need to be properly prepared. This may seem like a lot of work for something you may do only every few years, but there is a good reason. One of the major problems people have with trade-ins is; they are what dealers call "buried" or "upside down" in their units. These terms mean that they owe more on their rigs than what the unit is worth to a lender or RV dealer. Therefore, with each successive RV purchase, they must put out large amounts of cash in addition to their trade in. This is caused by a few pitfalls that you will want to, and can avoid. The first is paying too much for the unit and/or the price of the add-ons from the F & I Department that arranges the financing. Another reason is due to making small monthly payments based on financing an RV for too many years. Last but not least, making too small a down payment to begin with can also come back to haunt on a subsequent purchase.

As I said earlier, an RV should not be considered a financial investment. However, making the wrong moves on your first one can bury you for many years. Most RV dealers, however, don't want to bury you because they know if they do it's unlikely they'll ever see you again. Most times, you won't even realize you're buried until you are way down the road. However, some short-sighted salespeople will try to hit a home run for a big fat commission check. What happens to you after you leave the dealership is not their concern.

I cannot stress enough the need for a pre-planned approach before you spend your hard-earned cash. Much like a home, a long term loan at a high rate can mean paying almost double the RV's selling price. But unlike a home, which may appreciate in value, RVs do not, they depreciate. A good hedge is to simply pay substantially less than the asking price and be realistic if you are financing. This sounds easy, and it is, if you don't get swept up in the emotions of what many eager buyers see as their "Big Dream." Keep your cool, even when you find the right unit, and then let the negotiating begin. Do this and you will prevent your dream from later turning into your nightmare. (See "Negotiating the Deal")

NEW OR PRE-OWNED

There will rapidly come a point, early in the shopping process, when you must decide whether a pre-owned unit will serve you as well as a new one. There are pros and cons to both. The pros on buying a pre-owned RV generally come down to saving money. One of the "cons" is that many people believe that in buying a used unit they are buying someone else's problems. In some instances it's true. If this is your thought, there are a couple of things you can do during negotiations to minimize your risk. Since most pre-owned units are sold "as is," or with a very short warranty, insist that the unit has a full "PDI" (Pre Delivery Inspection). This basically means that the entire unit is gone through from top to bottom at the time of delivery to ensure all systems are in working order. This, most likely, will exclude cosmetic problems. Another item that you can negotiate into the deal is an extended service contract that covers items of concern. Another good idea when purchasing a used unit is to take somebody who is knowledgeable with RV's along with you. They can check the unit out and offer sound advice based on experience.

A very large negative if you choose to finance a used unit is the interest rate on the loan. Generally, the rate will be 15% to 25% higher on a used unit than on a new unit, and with fewer years to pay it off. When you find a good unit, the first thing to check out before negotiating on price is the N.A.D.A. Guide (Recreation Vehicle Appraisal Guide) www.nada.com

This is the "Bible" for most dealers, as it lists the selling price of any pre-owned unit and is also used for evaluating trades. It can be used for free on the internet, and can often be found in some public libraries. If you use a hard copy make sure it is a current issue. Prices change three times a year.

The other guide that you may hear about is the Kelly Blue Book. This is another good guide, however, the N.A.D.A. prices, which are published three times a year; tend to have lower prices than Kelly which is good for buyers of pre-owned units.

Now before you decide that a pre-owned RV is better than a new one because of its lower price, let's talk about new units. There are many benefits to buying new. For starters, you are the first to sleep in the bed and use the facilities, you have a full warranty from the manufacturer, and financing percentages are lower with longer terms. And, most importantly, you are in a better negotiating position. The reasoning behind the last point is simple - the dealer can always get another RV from the factory just like the one you're buying because the factory makes it day in and day out. Pre-owned units, on the other hand, tend to be "one of a kind." Later, we will cover special factory incentives, often quite substantial. As far as depreciation worries, forget them. Depreciation is figured from the MSRP, not the selling price. When you buy smart (and right) for at least 15% - 20% off the MSRP, you will be in good shape. By the time you finish this guide and put into practice what you have learned, you will be where you need to be for at least one year's worth of depreciation, possibly even two.

Note: Check out some of our other helpful RV buying tips at www.rvpublications.com

CHAPTER 4

INFORMATION GATHERING

Okay, so now you have read a few chapters and are ready to hop into your car and drive to your local RV dealer to wheel and deal and then hit the road. Fine, but for now, slow down: there is much more to learn. Unless you have already found the absolutely "perfect unit" and it's the last of its kind, hold up for just a little longer. Now that you have filled out your customer preference worksheet and have had some good conversations with your traveling partner, you are ready to put your plan together. If you have decided on a pre-owned RV, you may skip this section of the guide. On the other hand, if you are leaning in the direction of a new unit, then you have some necessary homework ahead of you. Now is the time for gathering information to make an informed decision. Later, if you decide on a pre-owned unit, this exercise will still have been worth the effort.

Gathering information about RVs can be done in several ways, depending upon how you want to go at it. It will vary a great deal based on where you live. If you are located in an area that has many dealers, pay them a visit and collect literature. Most manufacturers do an excellent job of providing prospective RV buyers with good product specifications through their network of RV dealers. This is the information you need at this point in the process. If you live in a more remote location, your information gathering will most likely be done by phone, mail or the Internet. The Internet can link you to the web sites of most major manufacturers, along with the specifications of their products. Be specific when you request literature about which product(s) you are interested in, and state that you are in a hurry to receive it. If you visit dealerships to get materials, avoid engaging in long conversations with salespeople. At this point, tell them you are just starting the shopping process and that you are probably a year away from buying. This should put them at bay.

If you are obtaining your information through the mail or the Internet, be ready to receive many letters from dealers about the brands in which you've shown an interest. Most manufacturers have what is called a "Hot Lead" card that they forward to the dealers after they receive inquiries for product information.

Another source of information that I did not mention is through RV consumer magazines, such as Trailer Life, Motorhome Magazine, Family Motor Coaching, etc. These publications offer information through what are called "Bingo" cards, located in the back of the magazine.

Use these cards to request information on many different products at one time. The only drawback to this method is that it generally takes weeks or even months to receive the information you request. However, no matter how you gather your material, eventually your living room or den will look like information central. This is okay, as the more information you possess, the better equipped you will be to make an intelligent purchase. Another place you will find information, are RV chat rooms on the net. However beware of the quality of the information.

In the next section, I will show you how to lay out a comparison guide so you can look at similar products in an "Apples to Apples" fashion. This will clear up all the hype found in brochures. But save the brochures so you can look at photos, illustrations, colors available and product specifications.

In the following section, you will need to put together a comparison checklist. As you will see, this can be as extensive as you wish. *The best way I have found to do this is to narrow down the field to the products that most closely match your preference sheet. After you have done this, use the RV you favor the most as the base unit.* This will allow you to get a true picture of how it stacks up against similar units. When narrowing your selection down, try as much as possible to select similar sizes and floor plans. Either way, the items listed on the left side should not change significantly as long as you stay with the same brand. The items listed on the left come straight out of the manufacturers' brochures in either the standard equipment or the options section.

I recommend that you leave the prices out until you are done. This will make it more objective. Remember, at this point, price is negotiable. Since we have not yet started to grind away at the asking price, let's not cloud things up. As I have stated, information gathering can be time consuming. It is best that two people work on this comparison checklist, one reading and one writing. This can be very enlightening and should open your eyes to the true value of a unit.

You will often find that a low MSRP is low because the unit omits many things that you may want down the road. This process is designed to work as a funnel for you, starting with all the choices you have, narrowing them down to the final choices of the serious contenders. **Use the Brand A and Brand B columns on the right side of the following charts to do your comparison shopping and to assist you in finding the perfect RV for you.**

COMPARISON SHOPPING GUIDE - MOTORIZED
EXAMPLE ONLY

CHASSIS

	BRAND A	**BRAND B**	**BRAND A**	**BRAND B**
Brand Name	XXXXX	YYYYY		
Price Leave Blank				
Type	Workhorse	Ford		
Engine HP/Torque	8100 Vortec 455lb-ft/340	Triton V10 457lb-ft/362		
Transmission	Allison 6-speed	TorqShift 5-speed		
Suspension	Parabolic taperspring	Tapered Multi-leaf		
GVWR	22,000 lb.	22,000 lb.		

CONSTRUCTION

	BRAND A	**BRAND B**	**BRAND A**	**BRAND B**
Roof	Wood	Laminated Aluminum		
Sidewalls	Wood	Laminated Aluminum		
Floor	Steel	Steel		
Compartments	Aluminum	Fiberglass		
Exterior	Smooth Aluminum	Gel Coat Fiberglass		

CAPACITIES

	BRAND A	BRAND B	BRAND A	BRAND B
Fuel Tank	75 Gallons	75 Gallons		
Fresh Water	75 Gallons	100 Gallons		
Gray Tank	45 Gallons	60 Gallons		
Black Tank	40 Gallons	50 Gallons		
LP Tank	28 Gallons	35 Gallons		
Water Heater	6-Gallon Gas/electric	10 gallon Gas/electric		
Refrigerator	8 Cu. feet	10 Cu. feet		
Towing	5,000 lb.	4,000 lb.		

MEASUREMENTS

	BRAND A	BRAND B	BRAND A	BRAND B
Length	35' 3"	36' 6"		
Road Height	11' 9"	12' 0"		
Int. Height	6' 4"	6' 6"		
Int. Width	96"	98"		
Ext. Width	102"	102"		
Wheelbase	218"	228"		
Unit Weight	18,900 lbs.	20,000 lbs.		

SLEEPING

	BRAND A	BRAND B	BRAND A	BRAND B
Master Bed	60" X 74"	60" X 80"		
Sofa	44" X 70"	48" X 72"		
Dinette	44" X 70"	46" X 70"		
Overhead	N/A	N/A		

SLIDE OUT

	BRAND A	BRAND B	BRAND A	BRAND B
Galley	N/A	N/A		
Living Rm.	15'	13'		
Bedroom	6'	N/A		

ELECTRICAL

	BRAND A	BRAND B	BRAND A	BRAND B
Amp Service	30 Amp	50 Amp		
12-Volt Bath Fan	Yes	Yes		
12-Volt Kitchen Fan	Yes	Yes		
Air Conditioner	2-13,500 BTU	1-13,500 1-11,000		
Front TV	19"	24"		
Rear TV	13"	19"		
DVD	Yes	Yes		
Video Control Box	N/A	Yes		

ELECTRICAL CONTINUED

	BRAND A	BRAND B	BRAND A	BRAND B
Satellite Sys.	N/A	Stationary		
Microwave	Yes	N/A		
Convection Oven	Gas Oven	Yes		
TV Antenna	Yes	Yes		
Coffee Maker	N/A	Yes		
Monitor System	Yes	Yes		
Generator	5.5 KW Generac	7.5 KW Onan		
Battery Disconnects	Yes	Yes		
Fluorescent Lights	Yes	Yes		
Reading Lights	Yes	Yes		
Porch Light	Yes	Yes		
AM/FM/CD	Yes	Yes		
Inverter	N/A	Yes		

EXTRAS

	BRAND A	BRAND B	BRAND A	BRAND B
Alternator	125 Amp	160Amp		
Aluminum Wheels	Yes	Steel Chrome		
Spare Tire	No	No		
Roof Rack/ Ladder	Ladder only	Yes		
Map Lights	Yes	Yes(2)		
Back up Monitor	Yes with Microphone	Yes/ no microphone		
Chrome Roof Horns	Yes	Optional		
Dash Fans	Yes	Yes		
Leveling Jacks	Optional	Yes Hydraulic		
Rosen Sun Visors	N/A	Yes		
Basement Storage	Yes	Yes		
Washer /Dryer	Optional	Yes		
Cell Phone Jack	Yes	Yes		
Wood Treatment	Oak/ Walnut	Oak/ Cherry		

EXTRAS CONTINUED

	BRAND A	BRAND B	BRAND A	BRAND B
Countertops	Corian	Formica		
Kitchen Sink	Stainless Steel	Porcelain		
Water Filter	Yes	yes		
Fabric Color Choices	Four	Three		

COMMENTS:

_____

_____

_____

_____

_____

_____

_____

_____

_____

_____

_____

_____

_____

_____

_____

_____

_____

_____

_____

_____

NOTE: If you're still not sure on what type of RV will best suit your needs, but have a general idea, it's a good idea to purchase a training DVD on the type RV you have in mind. This visual form of media will give you a much better idea if a particular RV is right for you and could save you a great deal of headaches and money before you make a purchase. RV training DVDs are available at www.rveducation101.com or you can use the mail-in order form at the back of this guide.

COMPARISON SHOPPING GUIDE - TOWABLES (EXAMPLE)
CHASSIS

	BRAND A	BRAND B	BRAND A	BRAND B
Brand Name	XXXXX	YYYYY		
Price Leave Blank				
Frame Size	6" C-Channel	8" C-Channel		
Tire Size	16"	15"		
# Axles	2	2		

CONSTRUCTION

	BRAND A	BRAND B	BRAND A	BRAND B
Roof	Rubber/ Wood	Vinyl/ Wood		
Sidewalls	2" Wood Frame	2" Aluminum		
Floor	2" Alum. 5/8 Ply.	2" Wood 5/8 Ply.		
Compartments	2-pass thru 2 non-pass	2-pass thru 4 non-pass		
Exterior	Fiberglass	Gel Coat Fiberglass		

CAPACITIES

	BRAND A	BRAND B	BRAND A	BRAND B
Fresh Water	40 Gallons	35 Gallons		
Gray Tank	35 Gallons	35 Gallons		
Black Tank	30 Gallons	35 Gallons		
LP Tank	2-7 Gallons	2-7 Gallons		
Water Heater	6-Gallon Gas/electric	6 gallon Gas only		
Refrigerator	8 Cu. feet	10 Cu. Feet / Icemaker		

MEASUREMENTS

	BRAND A	BRAND B	BRAND A	BRAND B
Length	32' 6"	33' 0"		
Road Height	10' 2"	10' 4"		
Int. Height	6' 4"	6' 6"		
Int. Width	94"	96"		
Ext. Width	96"	102"		
Tongue Weight	754 lbs.	560 lbs.		
Dry Weight	5,200 lbs.	4,500 lbs		
GVWR	6,700 lbs.	5,900 lbs.		

SLEEPING

	BRAND A	BRAND B	BRAND A	BRAND B
Master Bed	60" X 76"	60" X 80"		
Sofa	54" X 80" Hide-a-Bed	46" X 52" Jack Knife		
Dinette	44" X 75"	46" X 76"		

SLIDE OUT

	BRAND A	BRAND B	BRAND A	BRAND B
Galley	N/A	N/A		
Living Rm.	13'	13'		
Bedroom	6'	7'		

ELECTRICAL

	BRAND A	BRAND B	BRAND A	BRAND B
Amp Service	30 Amp	30 Amp		
12-Volt Bath Fan	STD	STD		
12-Volt Kitchen Fan	STD	Optional		
Air Conditioner	1-13,500 BTU	1-15,000 BTU		
L/R TV	25"	N/A		
B/R TV	19"	N/A		
DVD	Yes	N/A		
Video Control Box	STD	N/A		

ELECTRICAL CONTINUED

	BRAND A	BRAND B	BRAND A	BRAND B
Satellite Sys.	Optional	Optional		
Microwave	Optional	STD		
Convection Oven	STD	Optional		
TV Antenna	STD	STD		
Coffee Makcr	N/A	STD		
Monitor System	STD	STD		
Generator	Ready-STD Optional	N/A		
Battery Disconnects	STD	N/A		
Fluorescent Lights	STD	STD		
Reading Lights	STD	N/A		
Porch Light	2	1		
AM/FM/CD	Bose STD	Sony w/CD		

EXTRAS

	BRAND A	BRAND B	BRAND A	BRAND B
Wheels	Chrome Steel	Hubcaps		
Spare Tire	Optional	STD		
Roof Rack/ Ladder	STD	Optional		
Leveling Jacks	Optional	4-Manual		
Cable TV Hook-up	STD	STD		
Gas Stove	3-Burner	3-Burner		
Gas Oven	STD	STD		
Water Filter	STD	Optional		
Wood Treatment	Oak/ Maple	Oak		
Countertops	Formica	Formica		
Computer Desk	STD on this Floor Plan	Flip-up Table		
Washer/ Dryer	Ready- Opt	N/A		
Wardrobes	2-large in bedroom	1-large in bedroom		
Tub/Shower	Combo/ Both	Tub Only		

EXTRAS CONTINUED

	BRAND A	BRAND B	BRAND A	BRAND B
Fabric Color Choices	Two	Three		

Note: Understanding options that are available, and can be ordered by the dealer, can be confusing. Take the time to sit down with the dealer and review these many options so you can equip your RV exactly how you want it.

COMMENTS:

_____
_____
_____
_____
_____
_____
_____
_____
_____
_____
_____
_____
_____
_____
_____
_____
_____
_____
_____
_____
_____
_____

Note: Keep in mind that these are just examples, but you can quickly begin to see how units stack up against each other. This will be an important consideration once price becomes a factor. It is quite possible to eliminate one or more brands or models just by comparing them to what other brands and models have to offer. You can also make wiser decisions based on your likes and dislikes and what each model has to offer. Use the Brand A and Brand B columns on the right side to do your comparison shopping and assist you with selecting the RV that's just right for you.

CHAPTER 5

WHEN IS THE BEST TIME TO BUY?

There is no best time to buy. There are, however, better times to buy than others. Probably the worst time to buy or hardest time to negotiate is when most people do, during the months of May, June and July. This is the time of year when people's thoughts turn to the great outdoors and the best way to enjoy it. Of course, this often means in an RV. There are times within this three-month period, however, when you can still get a good deal. They are the last 10 days of the month, because most dealers run a calendar month as it pertains to their bookkeeping. Every business likes to maximize each month's sales and often times a dealership will offer incentives to pack the last few days of the month with deliveries. These days work during any month of the year. The months of August and September are excellent months to purchase year-end clearance units. As the new coaches start to arrive in August, the sales staff migrates to the new models and forgets last year's models, even though they, too, are still new. At this point, these units are considered a year old and you can look at the N.A.D.A. book to see what each will be worth the day it's driven or towed off the lot. The price in the book should be the starting point for negotiating, with the dealer invoice at the bottom of the range (more about invoices later).

The other nice thing about buying a current year model after the upcoming year's models have arrived are the manufacturer and dealer incentives. These can add up to thousands of dollars in cash rebates, shopping sprees, and discounted financing. The months of October, November and December are excellent months to negotiate on new current model year inventory, as they are the slowest for sales and the dealer is paying flooring (floor plan interest) charges. January though April are mediocre months, with January being the worst for the dealer. The reasoning behind this is people are waiting to buy at the spring RV shows. RV shows are a great place to see products, learn more about RV's and visit RV dealers, but they are not necessarily great places to buy an RV. This is due to the hype and false sense of urgency. You are far better to go into the dealerships two to three weeks after a show.

The dealer has taken many customers off the early market and knows the next six weeks will be slow. And you should never purchase from a dealer unless you have visited their physical location. You need to determine if they are established and can take care of you after the sale.

As I mentioned earlier, there are better times to buy than others, but shopping can be done at anytime. One of the things that dealers teach sales people is to create a sense of urgency. *Interest rates are going up, we anticipate a price increase from the manufacturer, you'll never find a better price than it is at this show, etc.* Think about it for a minute. If a dealer pays thousands of dollars to go into a show, and pays to advertise the show, how can it really cut prices? It can't - unless, of course, it has lots of room to wiggle between asking price and cost. Therefore, selling from the lot reduces the dealer's cost factor and it can discount more to move the unit. We will get into determining the cost in later chapters.

Note: RV manufacturers do in some cases offer incentives to help promote sales during show dates.

UNDERSTANDING THE SELLING PROCESS

The purchases we are happiest with are those we have "bought." But sometimes we are "sold" things. Believe me when I say there is a difference. When we buy something on our own, and it turns out to not be what we expected, we generally chalk it up to a poor decision on our part. But when we feel we were "sold" something and the same result occurs our response is generally much stronger. "That !@#$%* really put it to me! I'll never do business with him again!" In reality, what you are not telling yourself is that you didn't do your homework. You believed all that was said, and walked blindly down the aisle and said "okay." As I stated earlier, a large portion of this guide and the exercises you will be asked to do are to properly position yourself to profit from the buying experience. By profit, I mean not only avoiding paying too much, but also buying the "right" unit for you. The wrong unit will, indeed, cost you money. But, more importantly, it will cause you frustration. This is not what RVing should be about.

In a perfect world, you decide you want something, walk into the place selling it, explain your needs, and walk out feeling you purchased what you wanted for less than you expected to pay. In the real world, the owner of a business directs his salespeople to sell you what the company wants sold. Most RV dealerships carry only a few brands of products and usually only a few floor plans of each. Therefore, when you walk into a dealership, some of your needs and wants are not even available. *The secret of a successful salesperson is to control the selling process from the initial greeting and throughout the negotiating process.* This is what sales staffs are taught to do.

If they are successful, they do it each and every time. Your first goal is for you to become an informed buyer who knows what he/she wants. Your second goal is to learn how to guide the selling process to where you receive what you want or are willing to accept. Not what the salesperson wants from you! You will not try to "rob" the dealer. The dealer is entitled to, and must make, a "reasonable" profit. If dealers were not allowed to make some profit, they wouldn't be around to sell or service your unit. Armed with what you learn in this guide, however, you will never become the "home run" talked about in sales meetings for months to come. This could happen, or even worse, you could become buried so deep in your unit that you will forever have to pay list price in order to be able to trade again. Trust me when I say this happen every day in dealerships across the country.

When you are greeted at the dealership, smile and tell the salesperson you are prepared to be a buyer if you find the right unit at the right price. Once you have said this, you will have their attention. Then move onto your preference sheet. *By doing this, you are taking control from the very beginning. If the sales person attempts to lead you off track, keep bringing him back. If you cannot be in your comfort zone, then you are most likely setting yourself up to lose in the negotiation phase.*

SELECTING A DEALER AND A SALESPERSON

After you have narrowed down what you think you want via the information-gathering process, you need to find a dealer to work with. If you are fortunate, there is one close to you that carries what you think is the right unit. If this is the case, you are ready to proceed. If, however, you don't find a dealer in your local yellow pages, call the manufacturer of the RV you are most interested in to learn the location of the nearest dealer. The telephone number may also be on the literature you have received. Another good way to find dealer locations is on the Internet. If you cannot find a dealer close by, call the one that's the closest, even if it's some distance away. Often times the dealer will pay for your gas to entice you to visit its lot. Remember, settling for something that is not right for you will eventually cost you more than a tank of gas. If it is worth buying, then it is worth traveling a distance to find.

Note: We also offer a good list of RV manufacturer links for you to research at www.rvpublications.com

Okay, now that you have found the dealer with the product you desire, what's next? Most reputable dealers take pride in their dealerships, so be wary of a place that appears untidy. Also, just because a dealer is large and impressive doesn't mean you are going to pay more. And just because one is a small "Mom and Pop" operation with only one service technician does not mean that you will save money. What's important is the pride the dealership takes in caring for customers before and after the sale. If you know people who have purchased from a particular dealer, ask them how they were treated and if they can recommend a good salesperson. If you cannot get a personal referral, go to the dealership and simply trust your instincts. The first thing you should get is a warm welcome and an offer for help. If you don't get this sort of attention and respect as a hot prospect, imagine the treatment you'll receive after the sale. And don't be afraid to wander around the dealership a bit and ask questions, such as:

1) How long have you been in business?

2) How long have you been selling brands X and Y?

3) How well is your service department staffed and do you have certified RV technicians?

4) If I buy an RV here, what type of PDI can I expect at time of delivery?

5) What type of familiarization will I receive on the unit before I leave with my purchase?

It's also a good idea to call the local Better Business Bureau to see if there are any major complaints on file regarding the business.

Note: It's a good idea to purchase an instructional DVD on the type of RV you plan to purchase before your scheduled walk through. You will be better prepared to ask targeted questions and won't need to spend time on what you already understand. There is a large selection of RV training DVD's available at www.rveducation101.com or you can use the mail-in form at the back of this guide.

These questions illustrate to a dealer that you are a serious buyer. One of the first things you may ask is if it is okay to browse the lot by yourselves to look around. If you say that you are just starting the looking process, they will generally give you an overview of the dealership and how it is laid out. Or they may offer to take you around to meet with the sales department. This is when you most need to trust your instincts. Don't be intimidated by a sales person. At this point, he or she works for you.

If the sales person is not helpful or doesn't seem to know the product like he or she should or is too pushy, return to the showroom and ask to see the sales manager. Ask to be assigned a different salesperson.

Dealerships lose sales every day because of personality conflicts. After all, each customer is different. The dealer would much rather have you work with someone you are comfortable with than lose you as a customer. Don't pass up what could be the perfect unit for you just because you don't like the salesperson. You are the customer and, as such, are the reason that the dealership is in business.

Once you get with your salesperson of choice be friendly, but be sure of yourself. Explain what stage you are in the buying process, what homework you have done, and where you think you are in the decision-making stage. I assure you that most salespeople, when confronted with a customer who has some idea of what he or she wants, will welcome that person.

Keep in mind that salespeople earn their livings by selling products, not by giving lot tours. An informed customer is always welcomed because the salesperson feels they can go right to the product for a purchase. This is about controlling the process. At this stage, the salesperson should listen. So fire away with questions. They are there to help you make the right choice, not make the choice for you. Each of us is different and has different needs. If a salesperson starts pointing you to the "special of the day," stop him and say you will look at it, but first you want to look at what you came in for. Remember what I said earlier, any unit could be the "special of the day."

While you are out looking at the product that you believe is right for you, it helps to start dropping buying hints. There are many, but some of the more common ones can work for you as a way to gather information before the negotiations. Try something like "What type of discounts are you offering?" or "Are there any manufacturer rebates being offered?" or my own personal favorite, "What could I buy this for **today**?" If the salesperson is quick to give you a discounted price of, say, 10% to 15% before negotiating, then you now have a starting price to go down from. If you are sure the unit you have found is the one you want, than the next step is negotiating the price. However, make sure you have read the next few sections about how MSRPs are figured and how the desk works.

CHAPTER 6

HOW THE MANUFACTURERS' MSRP'S ARE FIGURED

To many of you, this chapter may contain the information that you purchased this guide for. For many years, as Director of Sales, a part of my job was to set both dealer and retail pricing parameters on our products. To truly understand how and why manufacturers come up with their percentages, you must first have a big picture of the negotiating process.

The RV industry is more than 50 years old and many veteran RV owners have been trading up for years. Once a typical customer purchases an RV, you can pretty well figure that the usual trading cycle will bring him back to the trading table in 6 years or less. You also have to figure that, with the exception of the very low-priced units, the RV owner has financed his purchase. As we will discuss in the finance section, your first few years of payments are generally being applied to interest, not principal. However, the depreciation does not take this into account. Therefore, the dealership has a dilemma: How does it show the customer some equity in the customer's trade when all he or she has paid is interest, and depreciation keeps moving the value down? The answer: The manufacturer gives the dealer more room to wiggle when working the trade in the form of a higher MSRP. If the customer has no trade, it gives the dealer more bargaining room to discount down from, or to make a larger profit. Obviously, you would want the dealer to come down in price to save you money. Of course, the dealer would rather not budge at all and maximize his profit.

Obviously, all trades are different; so all MSRPs cannot be the same. There are, however, some definitive patterns that most follow. Generally, RV owners don't take big jumps when trading up. For instance, a person with a tent camper would not normally trade up to a Class A diesel pusher. A more logical progression would be to move up to a travel trailer or possibly a Class C motor home. Therefore, when MSRPs are figured, the manufacturer tries to consider both the anticipated trade customer as well as the competition that the manufacturer is facing in the market place. *The rule of thumb is that the lower the price of the unit, the lower the percentage markup of the MSRP.* On a tent trailer or entry level towable, for example, it's about 30% over dealer cost. As the amenity level goes up, the person who is looking to buy is more likely to have more of a trade in, so up goes the MSRP.

When you get to the intermediate price towables level, the MSRP is about 35% over dealer cost. In motorized, the same logic is followed, so an entry level Class C or Class A will reflect an MSRP of 30% to 40% over dealer cost. As you get into non-entry level Class A motor homes, the MSRP can be 40%. *When I speak of entry-level products, I am referring to the very basics in a unit. In these types of products, you will generally find the standards list short and the available options list very long.* The idea here is to get you into a basic unit brand (to join the family, so to speak) and you will hopefully, stay with the manufacturer for life. Since the average RV owner will buy 3.5 new coaches in his or her lifetime there is logic in selling entry level product. This is called multi-level price marketing.

Therefore, you will often find that if you like the price of an entry level unit but plan to load it with options, you may be better off buying an intermediate level product with more standard features. *This is because options are generally figured at between 30% to 40% over dealer cost and will raise your entry level coach to a price as high, or higher than an intermediate level unit.* The "Loss Leader" philosophy of many dealers and manufacturers will get you in the door to look at a product, but many times won't fit your needs. But you did come in, didn't you? If you buy a base unit as it sits, you probably will be okay down the road at trade-in time. However, if you load it up with options, you most likely will be buried in the trade. A common fallacy with RV buyers is that any loaded unit will bring much more in trade. *In reality, most dealers give you the wholesale value (or less) of the unit no matter what the options are.* Remember putting on options is like home remodeling. What may be worth a great deal to you can have little or no value to others. So dealers go less by what the options are worth and mainly look only at what the base coach value is.

This next section is extremely important and you need to make sure you understand this. *When looking at the price of a new unit and trying to determine dealer cost, remember it is a percent <u>over cost</u> - not a percent off sticker.* For example: A coach, which cost the dealer $100,000 at 40% MSRP will show a price tag of $140,000 plus the dealers "PAC". **Do not figure it the other way**, where you subtract 40% from $140,000 or you end up with a dealer cost of $84,000, which is totally inaccurate. Also, as mentioned in this book's glossary, almost all dealers charge a "PAC" to cover operational sales costs. This profit they never give up.

However, they are willing to give up much of the MSRP as you will see in the following sections, either by providing an inflated trade in value or by offering a discount off the MSRP. Remember, they do have to make a reasonable profit to stay in business and service what they sell. I offer the information above so you have a benchmark for saving money and to prevent you from becoming buried at trade-in time. Please don't abuse it. All dealers like to make money and consumers like to save money. *If you can buy for 10% to 15% over cost, both you and the dealer should be happy.* Depreciation, as mentioned earlier, is figured off of MSRP, not from the price purchased. When you buy your RV, if you can walk away with the first year's depreciation covered, you are in good shape with basically a free year's worth of use. We will cover negotiating the deal in a later section, so don't jump up just yet to go shopping for you new RV.

UNDERSTANDING TRADE IN VALUES

If you are like many people reading this guide, you already have an RV sitting in your driveway that you plan to sell or trade for something bigger, smaller or just newer. The fact is if you want to buy another RV you will need to find a new home for the one you already own. There are really only two ways to do this: sell it as a private party or trade it in where you buy your new rig. Depending on your mind set, location, and tolerance for strangers, calling you at all hours, you will have to choose which is better for you. The question you should ask is "Which plan is financially better for me in the overall picture?"

First, let's look at how a dealer trades for your unit. *I'll warn you ahead of time, this may seem complicated at first, so read it twice or more until you fully understand.* Pull out a pad of paper, pencil and pocket calculator if necessary. This chapter is very important if you do have a trade in. An incomplete knowledge of the information I present here can be dangerous. If you go to a dealership without understanding where it's coming from, you may be in worse shape than if you were simply clueless. *Understanding what you are about to learn will give you incredible power and confidence! But revealing to the dealer that you have this knowledge is foolish. So just keep it between you and your purchase partner.*

Let's start with a hypothetical unit. Let's say you own a 1999, 33' gasoline-powered motor home with 55,000 miles on it. What is it worth? As I wrote earlier, go into the N.A.D.A. price guide. You will see two columns on the right, one for retail and the other for wholesale.

At retail, let's say it is worth $50,000, and at wholesale $40,000. If you sell it as a private party, retail is where you will start. Where you end up will be determined at how good a salesperson you are. So, if all goes well and you get a good price, and the coach is already paid off, then you will go shopping with a pocketful of money. If it wasn't paid off or you sold for a low price, you will walk into the dealer with less to plop down on the sales table.

In scenario #2, you decide to trade it in. After all, it's worth $50,000, right? Maybe. While someone could pay you the full retail price, it rarely happens. What will most likely happen is the dealer will <u>show you the trade's</u> full retail value as a trade in on his worksheet, and you'll be thrilled, and maybe even a little proud that you worked such a great deal. Alas, the dealer is not necessarily being overly generous: it's all in the MSRP. This is what is called the "trade value." It's the value over what the dealer is actually allowing for your unit as a trade in. What the dealer is most likely <u>assigning</u> as a value in his own mind is roughly the used RV's wholesale number of $40,000, or less. *The difference between the assigned value of $40,000 and the $50,000 that you are being shown (the $10,000) is coming out of the spread between dealer cost and MSRP price.* Say the coach you want to buy has an MSRP of $120,000. Using what we know about figuring cost versus MSRP, dealer cost would be roughly $85,000. Now let's say he wants to make $20,000 after cost. Cost plus profit totals to $105,000. Add to this the PDI and dealer PAC and total cost is now $108,000. Subtract what he has assigned to your coach, $40,000, and you have $68,000 as a trading difference. This is what you will pay the dealer, plus your trade. So you just bought a $120,000 unit for $68,000 and your trade that was worth $50,000 at full retail if you could have gotten it. "I got a great deal," you will think! Dealers like trade-in customers for the above reasons. They made $20,000 on the new coach and potentially can make another $10,000 from the sale of your used unit. *Had you pressed, the dealer would have very likely gone down on the new coach by another $10,000 to $12,000 so as not to lose the potential of a saleable trade.* After all, the dealer can pick up the phone and order another new RV just like the one you just bought. Many times, I have seen a dealer give up all profit on a new unit except the PAC and PDI costs just to get a desirable trade.

Remember, though, a desirable trade is in the eyes of the dealer, not the customer. The scenario above is a typical trade deal. As you can see, the MSRP gave the dealer a lot of flexibility. He can work it several different ways. If you had told the dealer that you still owed a substantial amount on your coach, he could have dropped the trade difference and shown the extra monies from the MSRP in additional trade value to show you with a greater equity balance. This is called an over allowance. This can help if you're financing and are buried in your old unit.

The other scenario would be walking in as a cash buyer. The unit cost is still $120,000 and dealer cost is still $85,000. When you add in the dealer PAC and PDI, the cost is still $88,000 before profit. This is the starting point for the dealer to work up from, and the final selling price above this - the allowed profit - is your part of the negotiating process.

HOW TO NEGOTIATE THE DEAL / HOW THE "DESK" WORKS

We should have learned much in the previous sections, if not please go back and read it again. You now should have the needed information to face the last, and possibly the toughest, phase in the buying process. You will find this to be a relatively short section, since the negotiation phase of the sale is only a small part of the process, albeit a very important one. *What you should have spent most of your time on is finding what fits your needs and price points.* Let us just recap for a minute where you should be in the cycle:

1) You have sorted through the information, researched and you know what you want.

2) You have determined who has the product and where you can buy it.

3) You have honestly appraised the value of your unit being traded in. (if applicable)

4) You have a ballpark idea of what the new unit's real costs are.

5) You have talked it over with your partner and are ready to BUY.

Now comes the time many of you may dislike intensely, and equate with a trip to the dentist, time to negotiate the price. Why? If you have followed the plan, you are very prepared to make this a money-saving opportunity and drive off in your "Means to the Dream." You have spent time with the sales person, you've asked all your questions about the unit that you are seriously considering, and you are comfortable with the responses.

You've told the dealer about your trade and implied you know what it is worth. You have a true idea of what you can expect at the time of delivery. So now it is time to march into the office. If you are trading, one of two things will happen at this point: the dealer will either start to write up the sale at the window sticker price or will ask if you are prepared to make an offer. At this point, announce that you will trade with them TODAY if the numbers are where you feel they should be. *You should have a good idea of where the final numbers will end up from doing your homework.* Tell the salesperson to write it up and you will give him an answer immediately, plus take delivery as soon as they can have the paperwork and unit ready.

To help keep them honest, also ask for their best cash price on the unit, since you have someone who might be interested in buying your old unit. This information gives the salesperson the proper motivation when he goes to the "desk" with your deal. When he goes into the "desk," the manager will ask many questions about you and the deal up to this point. One of the first questions will be about the trade if one is involved and your expectations of its value. Next will be whether you have discussed a trade difference or monthly payments. The manager - "the desk" - will work up the numbers and send the salesperson back to you. What you will most likely see is a number that you know is too high. But this is what the salesperson is paid for - to make a profit. Unless the numbers are what you expected, tell him they are not where you feel they should be. Get up, thank him for his time and start to leave. At this point, he will ask you to wait while he goes back to talk with the manager. What will most likely happen next is called the "T.O." (Turn Over). The manager will come in and basically ask what you feel are the "right numbers." Now is your opportunity to tell him. At this point, you will probably be told that there is no way the dealership can sell the unit for what you want to pay.

And then they will try to close you at the price originally presented. Ignore it. It might feel awkward to you but it is important that you just ignore it. Ask that they get back together and sharpen their pencils again, since you would prefer buying from them rather than go off to another dealer in search of the same unit.

The moment of truth: Preface your statement that you are a sincere buyer and will sign today for what you feel is a fair price for both parties. They will go back to the office and come back with another number closer to yours. If you still want more, but you're not far off, pause for a second and then ask to be left alone for a couple of minutes.

Then come back and offer what is called "a gentleman's split," which basically splits the difference between their revised offer and yours. At this point, you are probably destined to be the proud new owner of an RV. They may, however, tell you that you didn't see all the value in the unit to truly understand the price they offered, and that you should go back out with the salesperson. *Explain to them that you have done your homework and you feel you do, in fact, know the product and its value.* Again, ask them to go back and see if there is more room to negotiate or if there are any special incentives on this unit, since they can always order another unit just like it. Also, offer to take a new ordered unit with the same equipment at a price closer to what you want to spend since you do understand that they may have additional carrying cost on the unit they have on the lot. Believe me, the dealer most always wants to sell the lot unit first. *This back and forth maneuvering can go on for quite a while, and it is extremely important that you hold your ground. The first one to show weakness will be the loser in the end.* Remember, you always have the ability to end the negotiating by either saying yes or getting up and leaving.

CHAPTER 7

THE FINANCE DEPARTMENT

Okay, you've finally agreed on the price that makes you happy. You stayed with what you wanted to spend and you won the battle. ***Well, as the old saying goes "You may have won the battle, but you could still lose the war."*** If you have chosen to finance your new purchase, there are still a few things you need to be aware of. In the RV business, as in the automobile business, one of the greatest profit centers is often the financial department. ***We call this working the "back side" of the deal.*** It is commonplace for the F & I Department to generate more profit on the "back side" than the sales staff did up front during price negotiations. After you have agreed on price, you must go to the finance department to get the legal paperwork done. This includes registration, licensing, loan contracts, etc. This is where your next challenge begins. You will be asked how you want to pay for the unit, by cash or by financing it. After the finance manager figures the total price on your new RV, including taxes, registration, plates, etc., you will be asked how much you would like the monthly payment to be. At this point, if you elect to go blindly with the dealer's financing, you could end up adding many dollars to the price of your coach. ***NEVER offer what you want the monthly payment to be!***

The first thing you will need to do is give information for a credit application. Most good F & I people can tell at a glance what your credit worthiness is by the information you provide, if it's accurate. They will start to quote you payment amounts and terms. ***Make sure you are being told, up front, what the rates are.*** You might feel awkward again, but it's extremely important that you do this. By law, you cannot be asked to blindly sign without this disclosure. ***Again, borrowing money is like any purchase: you should always shop for rates and terms. If you have not done this before the purchase, you many feel obligated to take the dealer's rates since you have taken up so many people's time already.*** Ask who the lenders are (the dealer generally has several). Rates and terms will vary by lender, depending upon their competitiveness and your credit history.

If you have a rate from your credit union or bank when you walk in, you'll be in a much better position to negotiate the finance rate.

Did I say negotiate? Yes, I did. Much like purchasing the unit, you can also negotiate a finance rate. A dealer works for what is called "participation."

This is the difference between what the lender will lend money for versus what the F & I person can get you to agree to pay. This percentage can easily add up to a profit as large as or larger than that made on the unit you just purchased over the life of the loan. *If you agree to a rate higher than what you could find elsewhere, you may be giving back what you saved on the "front side" of the negotiating.* Should you finance with the dealer? Finance with whoever provides the best rates and terms, whether it be the dealer or your Aunt Matilda.

Let's talk a little more about interest rates. Interest rates affect what your monthly payment will be and the total amount of money you will pay for the RV if you keep it for the life of the loan. Keep in mind that buying an RV is considered a luxury item and you must have good credit to secure a loan, especially from the RV specialty lending banks. A bank will consider an applicant with an average credit history, but if you are approved it will be at a higher interest rate because the bank is taking a higher risk. The good news is that a good credit rating equates to good interest rates. I said a moment ago that any money you saved during the negotiating process could be lost during the financing process. RV lending banks offer RV dealerships competitive interest rates in an attempt to get the RV dealers loan business. The finance office will then offer you an interest rate in an attempt to get your business. If they get a higher interest rate from you than the bank offered them, they get paid what the participation. *Interest rates are something you must compare before you sign a bank contract.* Get a quote from one of the RV dealer's banks, one from your bank and one from an Internet lending source that finances RV's. *Find out what the current interest rates are and if you have above average credit don't settle for higher rates. It will really pay you to do your home work on interest rates before making the deal.*

RV FINANCING FREQUENTLY ASKED QUESTIONS

Will one RV lender offer better interest rates than another RV lender?

Interest rates change frequently. If the prime rate goes up RV finance rates will go up too. RV lenders send updated rate sheets to RV dealers whenever their rates change. RV specialty lenders watch each other closely and if one lender lowers rates the other lenders will generally follow suit. They will usually stay within a quarter to a half point of each other.

Are there other factors that will determine what interest rate I get?

Yes, there are several factors that will determine the rate you get.

1) It depends if the RV is new or used. A used RV (normally over 3 or 4 years old) will get a higher interest rate than a new RV will.
2) Your down payment will affect your interest rate. If you finance the RV on a zero down program the interest rate will be higher.
3) The term on the loan will affect the interest rate. The shorter the term the higher the rate, the longer the term the lower the rate.
4) The amount financed will affect the interest rate. The lower the dollar amount the higher the rate, the higher the dollar amount the lower the rate.
5) Your credit history (credit rating or score) will affect the rate. The better your credit score the lower the interest rate.
6) Carefully read the section on finance terms and interest rates in this chapter.

Should I shop around for a better rate, or will the rate they offer be the best rate I can get?

You should be aware of what the current rates are for RV loans and based on the criteria listed determine if you are getting the best possible rate you can get. If you think you qualify for a lower rate, by all means try securing a better rate elsewhere. There are several RV specialty lenders on the internet that would like your business and will offer competitive rates.

Do not however let too many lenders run a credit check on you to try and get a lower rate. This can backfire so be selective about who is running credit checks on you. If lenders make several inquires on your credit history your credit score will be lowered causing you to get a higher interest rate. The reason for this is when banks see numerous inquires they are under the impression that you are having trouble securing a loan and could be a credit risk to the bank. While we're on this subject, when the RV dealer is going to run a credit check on you make sure you tell them to only submit your application to one lender. Some unscrupulous finance people think it's easier to submit your credit application to all of the banks at one time, leaving you with numerous credit inquires.

Can you explain more about financing an RV with no money down?

There are usually a couple of lenders that will offer no money down finance programs. These programs will have certain guidelines to qualify. The type of RV, dollar amount, term of the loan and your credit rating can all factor into these types of programs. The finance rate will usually be higher too.

What length of term can I expect to get on an RV loan?

The term of the loan will be based on the dollar amount financed and the age of the RV. Some RV lenders are offering 20 year loans on financed amounts over $100,000 and loans ranging from $25,000 to $99,000 can qualify for 15 year loans. Loan amounts between $10,000 and $25,000 may qualify for 10 to 12 years loan terms.

Why would anybody want to pay the interest on a 15 or 20 year loan?

The biggest advantage of a long term loan is you get a lower monthly payment. Financing $100,000 for 240 months at 7% interest would be $775 a month. The same loan for 120 months would be $1,161 a month. You save almost $400.00 a month. But keep in mind you will have little or no equity if you try to trade within the first several years.

There are several things you need to consider when you determine what the best term would be for you.

1) How much can you afford to pay every month? The term of the loan directly affects the monthly payment.
2) How long do you plan to keep the RV? If you only plan to keep it for 3 or 4 years you won't be paying all of the interest anyway. The downside to this is you won't have any equity built up in it either.
3) If you plan to refinance the loan, or pay the loan off before the full term, a longer term loan would probably make more sense.
4) If you plan to keep the RV for the life of the loan a shorter term loan might be better for you. Make sure you can handle the higher monthly payments and the more you can put down initially the better.

Can I finance an RV with below average credit?

RV's are basically considered a luxury item, so the criteria to finance an RV are more stringent than it is to finance an automobile. There are lenders that will finance below average credit but interest rates will be higher.

How is the interest on an RV loan calculated?

The majority of RV loans from RV specialty lenders are simple interest fixed rate loans. What this means is you will only pay interest on the principle owed, and in most cases there is no penalty for paying the loan off early. If you choose to pay more than your required monthly payment you can shorten the term of the loan and save on interest.

Can I write the interest off on my income taxes?

Yes, a fully self contained RV is considered a 2nd home and all of the interest paid is deductible, if you are not already deducting the interest on a 2nd home. At the time of this writing an RV is considered a qualified residence if it is one of the two residences chosen by the taxpayer for purposes of deductibility in the tax year as long as it provides basic living accommodations, meaning it has cooking, sleeping and bathroom facilities with fresh water and waste water holding tanks. Talk to your tax advisor about what is required to write the interest off on your RV.

Will I need a down payment and if so how much?

Down payments will vary slightly between RV lenders but 10 to 20% down, in the form of cash or a trade-in, is usually the range. There are programs that offer low down, or no down payment but this will usually increase the interest rate. Most banks want to see your good faith commitment to the loan.

Do I have to have insurance on the RV to get a loan?

Yes, insurance is required when you close on the loan. The bank will not loan the money until they have proof of insurance.

Should I finance the RV or pay cash?

It is my personal opinion that it makes more sense to finance your RV purchase. If you finance the RV you can maintain your personal financial status without liquidating any assets. You can also take advantage of writing off the interest on your income taxes if the RV qualifies.

The above section covered the "F" in F & I. The "I" stands for insurance. If you are financing your RV, you may be required by the lender to have some coverage for its protection. Your state may also have specific insurance requirements. This information is available from the dealer, as are all types of wrap around service policies for either new or used products.

Are they profitable to the dealerships? Yes. In some instances, depending on the type of policy, a dealer can make 100% in profit. In addition to these basic policies, they may offer to sell you other goodies like fabric protectors, clear coat finishes, undercoating, and the like. All I can say about most of these last items is that they are seldom worth what you pay for them even less so if you're financing them and paying interest on them. If you look around in the yellow pages, you will find services that provide them, and usually at a more competitive rate than at most dealerships. Always get insurance quotes from other reputable insurance companies that offer specialty RV insurance, before you say yes to the dealer's carrier. Don't be afraid to ask to use the dealer's telephone to call for another quote. As I stated before, this is a profit center and you can and should negotiate a better rate than what you are quoted. As you are probably starting to see in this finance section, as in other parts of this guide, "being aware" is the best way to save money. The next chapter discusses RV insurance and extended service contracts in greater detail.

CHAPTER 8

RV INSURANCE

Content for this chapter was provided by National Interstate Insurance Company and Explorer RV Insurance Agency, Inc.

I have mentioned several times that your new or used RV is a major investment. To protect your investment you need the proper type of insurance coverage. There are several major insurance companies that specialize in RV insurance and I strongly recommend that you use one that does specialize in RV's. You might have a great insurance company for your home and automobiles, but an auto policy can't begin to cover the complexities of an RV. You need specialty coverage like vacation liability, total loss replacement, personal effects and much more.

When you insure your new motor home or travel trailer, the choices you have in insurance companies and coverage can be very confusing. The intent of this chapter is to explain the benefits and options you have with a specialty RV policy. To help make it easier to understand RV insurance, I divided this chapter into four primary sections. The first section discusses the basics of RV and auto insurance. This section will apply to you regardless of what insurance company you choose to go with. The second section explains additional specialty RV coverage that can be used to create a customized RV insurance policy to fit your needs exactly. The third section explains different valuation and loss settlement techniques that most RV specialty insurance carriers can offer you. The fourth section explains some effective ways to reduce your RV insurance premium and it provides some different ways you can buy RV insurance.

SECTION 1- RV AND AUTO INSURANCE BASICS

I know I just said that an auto policy will not suffice for an RV, but there is a great deal of overlap between RV and auto policies. If you have a motorized RV, you will need some of the same coverage's provided by an auto policy plus specialized RV coverage's. Bear with me and I will attempt to explain this without confusing you.

Regardless of the insurance company you decide to use, there are a handful of basic coverage's you will need to have in your policy. Again, this coverage is very similar, if not identical, to the coverage you have on your personal auto insurance policy. This coverage can be broken down into two different categories; liability and physical damage. All motorized

RV's will have some form of liability coverage. Towable RV's like travel trailers and 5ᵗʰ wheel trailers do not have any liability coverage.

However, if you own a travel trailer or 5ᵗʰ wheel the section on liability may contain information helpful to you regarding the vehicle you use to tow your trailer.

LIABILITY COVERAGE

There are a number of coverage's that fall under the category of liability coverage including Bodily Injury, Property Damage, Uninsured Motorist Bodily Injury, Underinsured Motorist, Uninsured Motorist Property Damage, Personal Injury Protection and Medical Payments. Some of these coverage's vary by state. I know this sounds confusing, but you'll have a much better understanding of liability coverage's after you read a brief generic description of each type.

Note: The Department of Insurance in the state you live in can be an excellent resource for additional information regarding state specific coverage's. Most states offer a Consumer Buyer's Guide on their website that will explain state specific nuances to each of these coverage's.

Bodily Injury is third party coverage. This means it provides protection for claims due to injuries to a passenger in your vehicle (other than you or a family member) or passengers in another vehicle, or pedestrians. It provides you, the owner/operator of a motor vehicle, with protection for your legal liability due to the ownership, maintenance or use of your RV. It is very important to select a limit that is high enough to protect your assets. You may be responsible for any amounts, related to injuries received to the third party, over and above the limit on your insurance policy. You can also purchase a separate umbrella policy that sits over all of your liability limits on your cars, your house and your motorized RV. This type of policy is not discussed in detail here, but provides protection above your Bodily Injury limit and up to the limit of the umbrella.

Property Damage is also a third party coverage, and provides protection for claims due to damage to other people's property. For example, Property Damage would pay to repair damage to the bumper of a car that you rear-end in an accident. **Bodily Injury and Property Damage** limits typically work together and can be either a split limit or a combined single limit. A typical split limit has a different limit for damages to each person, each accident and property damage.

For example, a common split limit would be $100,000 / $300,000 / $50,000. This means that for Bodily Injury coverage you have a maximum limit of $100,000 per person for each person injured not to exceed $300,000 per accident and a $50,000 limit for Property Damage.

A common single limit for Bodily Injury and Property Damage is $300,000 meaning you have $300,000 to pay for all injuries and property damage arising from any one accident. It can be split any which way between injured parties and damaged property. Bodily Injury and Property Damage are required for all motorized RV's. For travel trailers and 5th wheel trailers liability follows the unit towing the trailer, so Bodily Injury and Property Damage coverage's are not necessary.

Uninsured Motorists (UM) and Underinsured Motorists (UIM) coverage's can be first or third party coverage's. UM provides protection for injuries you or someone else sustains in an accident due to the fault of another party when the at-fault party does not have any insurance. UIM provides protection for injuries you or someone else sustain in an accident due to the fault of another party when the at-fault party does have insurance, but not enough insurance to cover your damages. UM and UIM are sold on a split limit and combined single limit basis, just like Bodily Injury and Property Damage.

Uninsured Motorists Property Damage (UMPD) provides protection for damage to your vehicle caused when your vehicle is struck by another party that does not have insurance. This would also be covered by Collision coverage, but UMPD typically has a lower deductible ($100 or $250) than the deductible on Collision coverage.

Personal Injury Protection (PIP) is also known as "No-Fault Coverage" and can be a first or third party coverage. This is a statutory coverage **that is only available in some states** and provides protection for injuries sustained in an accident regardless of fault. In a true no-fault state your insurer pays for your injuries, and the other party's insurer pays for their injuries regardless of who is at-fault. PIP benefits are state mandated and can include medical expenses, lost wages, funeral expenses and substitute services. If you live in a PIP state, you should consult your insurance agent or the department of insurance for more information on the PIP options and rules that pertain to your state.

Medical Payments can also be a first or third party coverage. This coverage provides protection for injuries of someone in your vehicle, including yourself, up to a specified limit. Medical Expense coverage is available in most states.

Liability Limits- When getting quotes on insurance, you will have to make several decisions about limits. You should pay close consideration to the liability limits you select. Liability coverage protects the insured in the event that the insured's negligence causes bodily injury or damage to property of others, and the insured is legally required to pay for damages.

Physical Damage Coverage- This would be a good time to talk about two of the common coverage's that fall under the physical damage section of the policy; Comprehensive and Collision. Comprehensive coverage is also commonly referred to as Other Than Collision. Comprehensive provides coverage for damage to your vehicle resulting from "other than a collision." Common examples are fire, theft, windstorm, hail, or flood damage. Collision provides coverage for damage to your vehicle that results when your vehicle strikes another object. Both of these coverage's are subject to a deductible, and for both coverage's raising the deductible lowers your premium.

SECTION 2- SPECIALTY RV COVERAGE"S

I mentioned earlier that there are a number of specialty coverage's available, designed to protect you and your property. **Specialty RV coverage's are what differentiates RV policies from auto policies.** Adding your RV to your auto policy is inadequate because it fails to cover many of the things included in a specialty RV policy. For example, most RV insurance provides coverage for awnings, furniture, permanently installed items and fixtures, and plumbing and electrical systems unique to RVs.

Typical RV policies also provide unlimited towing and roadside labor coverage. Auto policy towing coverage is often inadequate for RV expenses. With most auto policies, the towing reimbursement is usually on a per occurrence basis. Because the fees to tow an RV or to change an RV tire are much higher than the same for an auto, these fees often exceed the per occurrence limits on an auto policy.

Another consideration for RV owners is that they get the benefit of specialized claims service when they choose to insure their RVs with specialty RV insurance as opposed to having RVs put on auto policies. The adjusters assigned to claims by insurance companies with specialty RV products usually have expertise with RVs, losses to RVs, and settling the value of the loss. Let's take a look at some more of these specialty RV coverage's available to you.

- **Diminishing Deductible** – Under this coverage your physical damage deductibles could be reduced 25% for each claim free year you have with the company. After four claims free years, your deductibles would be $0. Any comprehensive or collision losses would reset the deductible.

- **Emergency Vacation Expense coverage-** is also unique for specialty RV policies. This provides coverage to pay for temporary living expenses if your RV is inoperable due to a covered loss and you are more than 50 miles from your home.

- **Vacation Liability** – Provides campsite liability for you while you are using your recreation vehicle as a vacation residence. For example Vacation Liability could cover damage caused by your campfire if it gets out of control or if you accidentally hit someone with a horseshoe.

- **Fulltimer's Coverage's-** This is very important coverage to insured's who use their RVs year round as their residence. There are three Fulltimer Coverage's available:
  - **Fulltimer's Personal Liability-** This provides personal liability type coverage to fulltime users of RVs, which usually equates to five or more months of use per year. This coverage is even available to individuals who do not own their own home, and is similar to the personal liability coverage on a homeowner's policy.
  - **Fulltimer's Secured Storage Personal Effects-** Many fulltime RVers keep some of their personal property in storage. With this option, the insured can get coverage for these items in storage. Typically, the insured will have to create a schedule of these items, and the insurance company will have specified limits for the value of this personal property.
  - **Fulltimer's Medical Payments-** This option provides coverage of medical expenses resulting from an accident that occurs while the vehicle is used as a permanent or primary residence. Insurance companies will likely require that the insured also has Fulltimer's Personal Liability coverage in order to qualify for medical payments coverage.

Note: Many insurance policies contain exclusions for using your RV as a permanent or primary residence. Often the Fulltimer's Liability endorsement removes these exclusions from the policy.

In other words if you are a fulltimer and do not carry Fulltimer's Liability you may be subject to policy exclusions.

- **Personal Effects** – provides coverage for loss to personal belongings used in conjunction with the RV.
- **Mexico Physical Damage Coverage**– Provides comprehensive and collision coverage for the insured vehicle while traveling in Mexico. The insured is required to purchase Mexican liability coverage too.
- **Mexican Liability Coverage-** While most RV insurance provides physical damage coverage while traveling in Mexico, it does not provide Mexican Liability Coverage. When traveling in Mexico by auto or RV, you must have Mexican Liability Coverage from a Mexican Insurance Company, which you can buy from US-based brokers or at the border.
  Type this link into your Internet web browser to read an informative article by Jim Labelle, about properly insuring yourself to travel south of the border.
  http://es1.mexicaninsuranceonline.com/press/mre_tm2003.html
- **Schedule Personal Effects Coverage**- Provides coverage for the loss of expensive personal belongings used in conjunction with the RV. The insured must have appraisals for these items.
- **Adjacent Structure coverage** may be available for storage sheds, screened rooms, or carports on owned or rented lots.
- In addition, you may be able to get coverage for roadside assistance, a utility trailer, a golf cart, or scooter.

SECTION 3- VALUATION & LOSS SETTLEMENT OPTIONS

There are several different physical damage valuation options that may be available to you when you insure your Recreation Vehicle. If you do not add any special coverage's that change the "default" valuation provisions in your policy you will have coverage on an Actual Cash Value (ACV) basis. ACV represents the value of the unit at the moment just prior to the loss. **In other words, ACV includes consideration for depreciation.**

- **Loss Settlement-** When you have a total loss to an automobile, the insurance company pays out the book value of the automobile, which is usually the N.A.D.A. (National Automobile Dealers Association) book value. However, because of the higher values of RVs and the effects of depreciation, a total loss can leave an RV owner with a payout far less than what is owed on the loan – leaving the individual to pay the remainder of the loan not covered by the insurance payout.

Note: Specialty RV insurance offers other loss settlement valuation methods that can protect you, the RV owner from the effects of depreciation.

- **Total Loss Replacement-** If your vehicle qualifies you may be able to purchase Total Loss Replacement (TLR) coverage for your policy. **This valuable coverage protects you against depreciation.** Typically if you have TLR coverage and your vehicle is a total loss during the first five years, the insurance company will replace your vehicle with a brand new vehicle. After the first five years, the valuation provision switches to a purchase price provision and you would receive the original purchase price of your recreation vehicle, so you are still protected against depreciation. In the event of a total loss of an RV, TLR coverage requires the insurance company to pay you the equivalent of a new unit of the same model, body type, class, size and equipment if you decide to replace your RV. You would have to replace your unit in order to receive this payout. If you choose not to replace your unit, you would only receive the actual cash value of your unit, which is basically the market value of the unit. Typically, this coverage is only eligible for the original owners of the RV. As you can see, Total Loss Replacement protects against the high costs of depreciation.

- **Purchase Price Guarantee-** This is another specialty coverage type that protects the insured against the effects of depreciation in the event of a total loss. Purchase Price Guarantee typically applies to the RV in its first 10 model years. In the event of a total loss, the insurance company will pay the insured the purchase price they paid for the vehicle. The Purchase Price Guarantee option is available instead of Total Loss Replacement when the vehicle is more than 5 years old but less than 10 years old, or if the vehicle is less than 5 years old, but the individual is not the original owner of the vehicle. A common stipulation with this option, however, is that the owner must have purchased the unit within the prior 12 months to be eligible for this coverage.

- **Agreed Value Coverage-** In order for Total Loss Replacement to work, the insurance company needs to be able to obtain a comparable replacement unit at the time of loss. Many RVs are difficult to value. For example, with custom bus conversions the market value of the unit cannot always be determined by the Kelly Blue Book, NADA or the bill of sale. There isn't such a market available for most custom bus conversions. Under Agreed Value coverage the insurance company and the insured agree on the value of the unit prior to the loss. The rating basis under Agreed Value coverage is based on the indicated market value of a qualified appraisal. These appraisals must then be updated every 3 years to substantiate the "Agreed Value". In the event of a total loss, the Agreed Value is paid to you. This option, however, does not fully protect against the effects of depreciation like Purchase Price Guarantee for Total Loss Replacement coverage's.

Now that you have a better understanding of how basic insurance coverage's work and how important it is to get specialty RV coverage, let's take a look at various ways you can reduce your insurance premium.

SECTION 4- WAYS TO REDUCE INSURANCE PREMIUMS

There are several ways you can reduce your insurance premium, including:

- Memberships in RV Associations
- Memberships in RV Manufacturing Associations
- Successful completion of driving safety courses
- Clean driving record
- Multi-Policy Discount (treated differently by each insurance co.)
- Improve your credit score
- Homeowners discounts
- Paid-in-Full discounts
- Adding a security device to your RV such as an audible alarm will often qualify for a discount.

Many insurance companies provide discounts to customers who are members of some type of RV association or club. Discounts vary by insurance company. Association discounts are often given for participants in RV manufacturing associations and clubs too.

Most insurance companies, including National Interstate Insurance Company will not stack discounts. As an example, even if you are a member of multiple qualified associations and you have taken a qualified driver safety course, the insurance company will most likely give you one 5% discount. A clean driving record can reduce your insurance premium. It usually takes 3 years (36 months) for accidents and moving violations/citations to stop impacting your insurance rates.

Another way to reduce your premium is to buy multiple policies from the same insurance company. This is called a multi-policy discount. As an example, companies like National Interstate Insurance Company offer discounts when an individual buys an RV policy and a companion auto policy. Homeowner's discounts are also common and some companies offer discounts if you pay in full up front.

HOW TO BUY RV INSURANCE

There are 3 primary channels for buying RV insurance:

- Through an Agent
- Buying Direct
- Online Quote Services

Through an Agent -Agents represent insurance companies and act as an intermediary between insurance companies and the consumer. There are two different types of agents:

Captive or Exclusive Agents- These are agents like State Farm agents who represent a full range of products from one carrier. These agents will usually only sell insurance products from one carrier. As an example, a State Farm agent will only sell State Farm products.

Independent agents- These agents typically represent a variety of insurance companies. Therefore, they have the ability to generate competitive quotes from several insurance companies. Independent agents can provide more insurance options for a consumer and help match the consumer's unique needs and preferences with an appropriate insurance option. For example, Explorer RV Insurance is an independent agency that sells products of National Interstate Insurance Company, Great American Insurance Company, Drive Insurance from Progressive, RLI, PersonalUmbrella.com, and several others.

Buying Direct- More and more insurance companies are selling directly to the consumer rather than through agents. Examples of companies doing this are Progressive Direct, and GMAC. Many consumers prefer the independence of shopping for insurance themselves and have a greater comfort level purchasing insurance this way. Many first-time RV insurance buyers, however, prefer the counsel of an agent.

Online Quote Services- There are an increasing number of online quote services that help match consumers and insurance providers. As an example, U.S. Insurance Zone www.usinsurancezone.com enables consumers to get quotes. These online quote services don't sell insurance directly, but facilitate a relationship between interested consumers and insurance providers. In other words, they help match buyers and sellers of insurance.

RV owners can find RV insurance through many RV dealerships and some RV associations too. Some of these organizations have their own internal insurance agencies and licensed agents which enables them to sell insurance policies. Other dealerships and associations have formal referral relationships with insurance agencies or insurance companies that sell direct.

Commercial Usage of RVs-If you want to lease/rent your RV, you will first want to explore your insurance options. The cost of insurance for having rental coverage can be very high and few insurance companies offer it. If you rent your RV without such coverage's, however, there are usually exclusions in your RV policy that prohibit such use. Therefore, if a renter has an accident or causes damage, your insurance company will most likely deny the claim.

If you intend to use your RV for other business uses, such as a mobile hotel, an onsite business location, a mobile service business, or other sales-related uses, the RV must be under a commercial policy. Most commercial vehicle policies do not have specialized RV coverage's. A few companies, such as National Interstate Insurance Company, offer a commercial policy for RV's used in business.

Note: To discuss Specialty RV Insurance Coverage, or to get a quote on RV insurance from Explorer RV Insurance Agency, Inc. call:

1-888-774-6778.

www.explorerrv.com

CHAPTER 9

EXTENDED SERVICE CONTRACTS

Content for his section was provided by RV Education 101

We talked earlier about how the finance department can also make money on the deal. One way was through the interest rate. Other ways are through selling you extended service plans, various insurance policies, tire guard plans, paint protection and more. It will be up to you to decide if these extras are worth the price. I do think extended service plans are great as long as you understand a little about them and how they work. When you are doing the finance paperwork on your RV most RV dealers will offer some type of extended service plan that you can purchase. Before you agree to purchase a plan make sure you understand all of your options. *Do not be pressured into buying an extended service contract.*

If you buy a new RV and purchase an extended service plan that covers both the coach and the chassis the plan would take over the day after all of the original factory warranties expire. For example, if you purchase a seven year extended service plan and the motorhome has a one year warranty on the coach and a three year warranty on the chassis the service plan would be in affect for six years after the coach warranty expires and for four additional years after the chassis warranty expires. The advantage of purchasing the plan when the RV is new is that it will be less expensive for a new unit as opposed to a used unit. Most plans can be purchased anytime up until the factory warranties expire if you don't purchase the plan when you initially buy the RV. Some extended service plans will offer coverage on used units that meet the plans criteria, if you purchase the plan when you buy the used unit. Coverage on a used unit will cost more. It is usually based on the age of the unit and the mileage if it's a motorized RV.

I mentioned if you buy coverage for the *coach and the chassis*. That's because most of these service plans offer different levels of coverage. You may only want additional coverage on the coach portion or on the chassis portion. In addition to different levels of coverage, plans are available for different terms.

Make sure you read and understand the extent and time period of coverage before signing any agreements. If you don't understand something, ask to have it explained to you. You will also want to make sure that the company offering the plan is reputable and will be acknowledged by other RV dealers and RV repair centers. It should offer coverage in all of the USA and/or Canada.

If you plan to travel outside your country of origin make sure the coverage is still available. You will also want to check on how a claim is paid. I have seen cases where you pay for the repairs up front and then get reimbursed when you send in a copy of the service order or repair bill. If the repair facility agrees to file the claim most plans only require that you call for approval before any repairs are made. *A good plan should be transferable if you sell your RV, it should be renewable so you can extend the coverage and it should offer a pro rated refund if coverage is terminated during the term of the contract.*

Pricing for these plans will be based on several factors. I have already mentioned some, the length of the plan, the extent of coverage, if the RV is new or used, the age and mileage, and the deductible. The deductible can range from 0 to over $200. This is not bad considering a $500 or $1,000 average repair bill if an appliance fails. Some items on the RV, like slide outs and entertainment systems may not be covered unless you pay an additional surcharge. Make sure you understand what these items are and if you want them to be covered by the plan.

Do not be pressured into purchasing a plan. Ask your RV dealer to give you a price on the plan they have to offer and then you can shop around and compare pricing for extended service plans. Just make sure the plans you are comparing offer similar coverage. There are reputable extended service plans available through RV clubs and on the Internet.

Note: Research and know in advance what you plan to do about an extended service plan before you go in to sign the finance paperwork.

EMERGENCY ROADSIDE ASSISTANCE

Don't get an extended service plan confused with an emergency roadside assistance plan. Some service plans do offer additional coverage and protection like a towing service or tire repair service, but most don't. Many RV manufacturers include an emergency roadside plan for a certain time period when you purchase a new RV. If the RV you buy does not come with one, I recommend you look into and purchase a good roadside assistance plan. It can be the difference between a good vacation and a ruined vacation. This is something else you will want to shop around and compare prices on before you buy. RV clubs offer discounted rates to members and there are many plans to choose from.

TAKING DELIVERY - "EXPECTATIONS AND REALITIES"

Well, you are past most of the challenging parts of the process and down to taking the unit home and making those first few trips. Generally, this is and should be the best part of the process. Yet, like anything new and built by humans, your new RV is bound to have a few bugs. So don't feel you have bought a lemon if you end up with a few things that don't work quite right. Most good dealerships will put your unit through a very comprehensive PDI process before delivery, which should catch most problems. PDI, as mentioned before, means pre-delivery inspection. The dealer's service technicians should check every item on the unit to ensure that all aesthetics and functions perform as the units' manufacturer intended them to (if it's a new unit). When you return to take delivery, there will be some additional paperwork to sign. But don't sign until you have thoroughly inspected the unit and have had your "walk through." A "walk through" is a familiarization orientation that should always be performed on a unit, whether new or pre-owned. Not only will you know that all is functioning as it should, you will also know how to operate everything on the unit.

Although most manufacturers provide some type of owner's manual, these publications vary greatly in their thoroughness. Most people like to feel and touch rather than just read about how something works. If the dealership's philosophy is "throw them the keys," you are in big trouble. Chances are that the salesperson explained the PDI and walk around procedure in your earlier visits. So it's now time to insist that they be as good as promised. You will feel far more confident that you can handle the unit after delivery.

Another benefit that some dealerships offer is the opportunity to spend your first couple of nights "camped" at the dealership. That way if you cannot remember something the next day, you are close by to get an answer. Also, if something malfunctions you are right there to have it fixed quickly. If the dealer doesn't offer an overnight stay your first night, a "shakedown trip" close to home (or the dealership if it is far from where you live) should be in order. If all goes well, you have lost nothing. If something does malfunction, then you are close enough that you can return to have warranty work done.

As I started out saying earlier, RVs are made by man and are subject to the same types of problems as any other mechanical product. However, they have thousands of parts and will travel all types of terrain. Problems can be expected and that is why manufacturers provide a warranty.

If you are taking delivery of a pre-owned coach, the same rules apply, except most are sold "As Is." So on pre-owned units make sure everything agreed upon has been completed to your satisfaction since once you are on your way; you have very little recourse about free fixes on any problems that come up. *Many times pre-owned coaches only carry the 50-50 warranty - 50 feet or 50 seconds- so be sure all items work as promised before you leave.*

Note: I recommend you purchase an instructional DVD for the type of RV you are interested in prior to taking delivery of the unit. This way you are better prepared to ask targeted questions during the walk through and you will already have a good understanding of how the RV is equipped and how the onboard systems operate. Instructional RV DVD's are available at www.rveducation101.com or you can use the mail-in form at the back of this guide.

BUYERS SHOPPING NOTES:

EPILOGUE

Well, you have finished reading this guide and are as ready as you will ever be to go out and start the RV buying process. I hope you feel the time spent reading this guide has been worthwhile. **_Remember, knowledge is power._** If you are a first-time buyer, you may still feel overwhelmed, even with the knowledge you have learned within these pages. I would recommend you give yourself a couple of days and read this over again. **_Buying an RV is the worst part of owning one._** Once you have the sales process behind you, you will find that, much like any other experience, you have learned a great deal. What I tried to focus on in this guide is the preparation aspect of the RV purchase. As I have stated many times, **_the preparation is what will make the end result satisfying._** If nothing else, you should be able to do two things that are critical: Get the "right" RV and not get hurt in the pocketbook. If you have already done your homework, know what you want and that it fits all your needs, than the information on pricing and negotiating is all you really needed to finish your mission - buying an RV. **_One last word of caution, Knowledge is indeed power...tipping your hat too much that you have it can backfire against you. Use the knowledge you have to win ...sharing it during the process can cause it to be turned against you by a savvy salesperson....I know...I've trained many._**

If you honestly feel this guide has or will help you, please urge anyone else you know who is planning to buy an RV to buy a copy themselves by visiting http://www.rvpublications.com. What I have shared with you here is the behind the scenes knowledge that I have learned through my life's work - the facts without the fluff. It has been 25 (plus) years in the making and I have quite a few more to go before we can hit the road to live our own dreams of exploring this great land.

So get out there and put what you have learned here to good use. And then start enjoying your new RV lifestyle. I'll see you down the road.

Good Luck and Good Shopping

Bob

LEGAL

This publication, RV Buyers Survival Guide, is the copyrighted property of RV Savvy Productions Inc. and may not be copied or reproduced by any means, whether electronic or otherwise, without express written permission of RV Savvy Productions Inc. Any distribution of copies or sections of this guide by any means, electronic or otherwise, will constitute an infringement; as covered in our 2007 copyright.

More Legal Stuff. . . . .

DISCLAIMER:

This program is provided "As Is" without warranty of any type, either expressed or implied.   RV Savvy Productions Inc. makes no representation, or warranties with respect to the contents hereof and specifically disclaim any implied warranties of merchantability or fitness for any particular purpose. In no event shall RVpublications.com be liable or responsible for any loss or damage, including, but not limited to any loss of profits, interruption of service, loss of business, or other incidental or consequential damages arising from the use or inability to use this product even if RV Savvy Productions Inc. has been advised of the possibility of such damages, or for any claim by any other party.

ISBN 0-9776025-3-2

RV Education 101

To order by FAX, include credit card information and FAX to 910-484-8276
To order by mail, fill out form and send it, along with payment to:
RV Education 101
3969 Stedman Cedar Creek Road
Fayetteville, NC 28312
Phone 910-484-7615
www.rveducation101.com

✓ **Method of Payment**   **Check**_____   **Credit Card**_____

Name_____ Date_____

Address_____ City_____ State____ Zip_____

Phone_____

Credit Card Orders: Visa____   Master Card____   American Express____

Name on Card_____ Card #_____

Expiration Date_____ Signature_____ Date_____

Use this form to order DVDs. For VHS and book orders please call or use our website.

DVD Titles	✓ Quantity	Amount
Pop-up		
Travel Trailer/5th Wheel		
Type A Motorhome		
Type C MH Rental/Owner		
Trailer Towing & Backing		
Towing Behind a Motorhome		
Winterizing & Storing Your RV		
Recommended Essential Items		$6.95 each
RV Campground Basics		

S&H $4.95 1 item / $7.95 2 or more items   **S&H**_____

DVDs $24.95   **Total**_____

RV Education 101

To order by FAX, include credit card information and FAX to 910-484-8276
To order by mail, fill out form and send it, along with payment to:
RV Education 101
3969 Stedman Cedar Creek Road
Fayetteville, NC 28312
Phone 910-484-7615
www.rveducation101.com

✓ **Method of Payment**   Check_____   Credit Card_____

Name_____ Date_____

Address_____ City_____ State_____ Zip_____

Phone_____

Credit Card Orders: Visa_____ **Master Card_____ American Express_____**

Name on Card_____ Card #_____

Expiration Date_____ Signature_____ Date_____

Use this form to order DVDs. For VHS and book orders please call or use our website.

DVD Titles	✓ Quantity	Amount
EZ RV Upgrades		
RV Care & Maintenance		
Deep Cycle Battery Care & Maint		
RV Safety Features & Tips		
RV Awning Use, Care & Maint.		
The RV Book		$19.95
The Insiders Guide to Buying an RV		$15.95

S&H $4.95 1 item / $7.95 2 or more items   **S&H_____**

DVDs $24.95   **Total_____**